This is a rare book on a vital subject; the key that unlocks the power of prayer is invariably the promise of God. Tom Yeakley shows us how to activate God's will in our lives and in the world around us.

PETE GREIG
Author, *Red Moon Rising* and *God on Mute*

If you've ever felt like the promises of God are unattainable or inapplicable to you, read this book. Tom Yeakley encourages us to boldly pray the promises of God. Your faith will thrive as you dare to believe, trust, pray, and prove the promises of God. As a result, I believe you will see God do immeasurably more than you could ask or imagine in your life and in the lives of those around you!

BECKY HARLING
Author, *Freedom from Performing* and *The 30-Day Praise Challenge*

This book is a treasure trove. A collection of God's promises. A library of stories. All a reminder that prayer need not be a hard task but a joyful experience of holding on to what God promises for you.

MARK BATTERSON
New York Times bestselling author of *The Circle Maker*

PRAYING OVER GOD'S PROMISES

The Lost Art of Taking Him at His Word

THOMAS R. YEAKLEY

A NavPress resource published in alliance
with Tyndale House Publishers, Inc.

NavPress is the publishing ministry of The Navigators, an international Christian organization and leader in personal spiritual development. NavPress is committed to helping people grow spiritually and enjoy lives of meaning and hope through personal and group resources that are biblically rooted, culturally relevant, and highly practical.

For more information, visit www.NavPress.com.

Praying over God's Promises: The Lost Art of Taking Him at His Word

Copyright © 1994, 2007, 2012, 2015 by Thomas R. Yeakley. All rights reserved.

A NavPress resource published in alliance with Tyndale House Publishers, Inc.

NAVPRESS and the NAVPRESS logo are registered trademarks of NavPress, The Navigators, Colorado Springs, CO. *TYNDALE* is a registered trademark of Tyndale House Publishers, Inc. Absence of ® in connection with marks of NavPress or other parties does not indicate an absence of registration of those marks.

Designed by Beth Sparkman

Cover photograph copyright © by Mikhail Dudarev/Veer. All rights reserved.

Cataloging-in-Publication Data is available.

ISBN 978-1-63146-378-5

Printed in the United States of America

21   20   19
7   6   5   4   3   2

To

Dana,

my wife and best friend,

whose trust in the promises of God

is a constant source of encouragement

and strength.

Contents

Preface

THERE ARE NUMEROUS BOOKS on the market about the topic of prayer and no small number on God's promises in the Bible. However, the number of books on claiming God's promises in prayer is much more limited, and to my knowledge there is no other book available that develops the concept of *pleading* God's promises in prayer. In fact, to find a book that takes an approach at all like this book's, we have to go back more than a century (see my limited bibliography).

Praying over the promises of Scripture has been a distinctive of the ministry of The Navigators, of which I am a part, since its origins in the 1930s. So it's fitting that NavPress would publish a book on this important and often neglected topic.

This book is written for a general Christian audience but not necessarily for new believers. It is *not* a basic book on how to pray. Rather, it is a call for followers of Christ to deepen their prayer life as they see God faithfully answering prayers based on the promises of Scripture.

To you whose prayer life is dull or empty, this book is designed to help revive and add vitality to prayers that seem powerless.

To you who are currently growing in your prayer life, I hope this book will encourage you to trust the Lord even more and to continue to grow in your faith.

Acknowledgments

MANY HAVE CONTRIBUTED DIRECTLY and indirectly to the writing of this book. Without their encouragement, critique, and examples, this book would not have been possible.

Special thanks go to my wife, Dana, and our three children: Michael, Amy, and Stephen, who have been fellow adventurers in our walk by faith. They have seen how the Lord is faithful to His promises.

I would also like to thank Lee and Debby Maschhoff, whose many hours of investment in our lives laid a good foundation upon which others were able to build. Their walk by faith, based on the promises of God's Word, remains a model and a challenge.

Thanks also to Badu and Wati Situmorang and the rest of the Indonesian Navigators staff, who have always demonstrated love and encouragement to me and my family. And thanks to the United States collegiate Navigators staff, whose ministries continually challenge my own faith as they live and minister from the promises of God.

And finally, I would like to express my deep gratitude to the generations of fellow Navigators who have gone before me. They have left a rich inheritance of faith in the promises of Scripture, from which I continue to draw inspiration and courage. I agree with Jesus' summary to His disciples: "Others have done the hard work, and you have reaped the benefits of their labor" (John 4:38).

Introduction

His divine power has given us everything we need for life and godliness
through our knowledge of him who called us by his own glory and
goodness. Through these he has given us his very great and precious
promises, so that through them you may participate in the divine
nature and escape the corruption in the world caused by evil desires.

2 PETER 1:3-4

AN OLD PROVERB STATES, "Promises are like pie-crusts, lightly
made and easily broken." Though this may be true concerning the promises of men, the same cannot be said concerning the promises of God. God's Word is always trustworthy
because it is founded on the character and power of God
Almighty.

The Christian life begins by trusting the promises of God,
such as "I tell you the truth, whoever hears my word and
believes him who sent me has eternal life and will not be
condemned; he has crossed over from death to life" (John
5:24). Or "My Father's will is that everyone who looks to the
Son and believes in him shall have eternal life, and I will raise
him up at the last day" (John 6:40). Or "I am the light of the

world. Whoever follows me will never walk in darkness, but will have the light of life" (John 8:12). By putting our trust in these promises and others like them found in the Bible, we obtain forgiveness for our sin, having been born again (2 Corinthians 5:17). After trusting Jesus as our personal Savior, we are given the Holy Spirit to live within us, helping us live the godly, Christian life (Romans 8:9). We become children of God (Romans 8:15-16; Galatians 3:26) and are made alive with Christ (Colossians 2:13).

The time when I called upon the Lord to keep these promises started during my third year of college. I was sitting in a dorm lobby at Florida State University waiting for Dana (now my wife) to come downstairs for a movie date. I looked across the lobby and saw a man with whom I had played football seven years earlier. We reintroduced ourselves and began to catch up on our lives but were cut short when his date arrived. After brief good-byes he headed off.

Upon reaching the lobby door, he turned and came back to me, pulling a small booklet out of his pocket. "Tom," he said, "I'm sorry I don't have time to explain this to you, but I wish you would read this booklet. The message in here changed my life." I thanked him, and off he went. I have not seen him again since.

That night before the movie began, I pulled the booklet from my pocket and read about God's plan of salvation. For the first time in my life I understood God's promises for forgiveness and eternal life through Christ. And there in that theater I claimed in prayer God's promises related to salvation, acknowledging my sin and my need for a Savior and trusting Him for His forgiveness and eternal life. That began a lifelong adventure, praying over God's biblical promises and trusting Him to keep His word.

Just as the Christian life begins by trusting the promises in God's Word, if we are to live the life God intends, we must continue to base our lives upon His promises. For many believers, the Christian life is one of mediocrity and spiritual dullness. The reality of a personal relationship with the holy, infinite, eternal Creator of the universe seems to have little impact on their daily existence. Their problems and trials seem insurmountable, and prayer becomes a formality or a "spiritual talisman." Where in this experience is the spiritual vitality of a living union with the risen Christ?

The Puritan pastor and author Samuel Clark (1684-1750) wrote in the introduction to his *Scripture Promises*:

> A fixed, constant attention to the promises, and a firm belief of them, would prevent solicitude and anxiety about the concerns of this life. It would keep the mind quiet and composed in every change, and support and keep up our sinking spirits under the several troubles of life. . . . A thorough acquaintance with the promises would be of the greatest advantage in prayer. With what comfort may the Christian . . . enforce his prayers, by pleading the several gracious promises![1]

Referring to the preceding quotation, J. I. Packer, in his modern classic *Knowing God*, writes,

> These things were understood once; but liberal theology, with its refusal to identify the written Scriptures with the Word of God, has largely robbed us of the habit of meditating on the promises, and basing our prayers on the promises, and venturing in faith in our ordinary daily life just as far as the promises will take us.[2]

Historically organizations such as The Navigators have talked about "claiming the promises" to mean placing our trust and faith in God and asking Him to do for us as He has promised in His Word. Today I would suggest a more accurate and biblical term is "pleading the promises." *Pleading* has a twofold meaning. One meaning is the sense of "pleading a case" in court, which implies the logical (and sometimes emotional) presentation of facts to make one's case. When we "plead" a promise in this sense, we're bringing God's own words before Him and saying, "God, You promised this. That's a fact. Please do for me as You have promised."

But just as a lawyer before a judge should be humble and respectful in view of the judge's authority, so also we must state the facts of God's promises with humility and respectful reverence. Though we boldly ask, we humbly submit our wills to His will. Holding God to His word doesn't imply disrespect or a demanding attitude. That's why we must also note the second aspect of the word *plead*—namely, "imploring" or "begging," which should elicit from us a bowing-to-the-ground attitude of humble submission.

The purpose of this book is to call believers back to prayer—specifically, back to praying over and pleading the promises of God. This habit of regularly reminding the Lord of His promises to us in prayer will bring vitality to our prayer lives and increase our faith as we see the Lord's faithfulness to His Word. Many have lost or neglected this habit, but God always stands ready to demonstrate His reliability and faithfulness. May we be quick to recognize our great loss and begin today to correct our neglect. Let us learn once again to pray over the promises!

1

WHAT IS A PROMISE?

There is something more necessary than the effort to exercise faith in each separate promise that comes to our attention. That is the cultivation of a trustful attitude toward God—the habit of always thinking of Him, of His ways and of His works, with bright, confident hopefulness. In such soil alone the individual promises take root and grow up.

ANDREW MURRAY

IT HAD BEEN A HECTIC DAY. The phone started ringing at six in the morning and I had been going nonstop since. Meetings with people—comforting some and exhorting others—had filled my day, and now I was ready for some time alone to relax and recharge my mental and emotional batteries. The delicious dinner was just settling and I had begun to look for some interesting reading material when my daughter, Amy, approached me and said, "Well, Dad, what game are we going to play tonight?"

I groaned inwardly and tried to plead some excuse about being tired, but to no avail. Her entreaties were now joined by the chorus of her two brothers, Michael and Stephen, all suggesting possible activities for our family fun night. Still I was slow to respond to their enthusiastic suggestions, thinking more of my own needs than theirs, and they were quick to perceive my reluctance.

"But, Dad, you promised!" they said in unison.

They were right; I had promised to spend the night playing with them, and they had the right to expect me to comply with that promise. Remembering that the image children have of their heavenly Father is formed to a great extent by their relationship with their earthly father, I put down my reading material and enjoyed an evening playing Monopoly with my family.

The Bible contains God the Father's promises to His children, along with other types of teaching and guidance to help us come to know and serve Him better. In fact, there are three main types of Bible content that we should note in our personal devotions and Bible study times: commandments, principles, and promises. These are given to us that we might know more of God's character and that we might demonstrate this character in our daily lives.

Commands, Principles, and Promises

Let's look briefly at each of these categories and consider how to apply each one to our lives.

Commands are God-given laws and instructions. They demand obedience from us. The most well-known are the Ten Commandments (Exodus 20). Other examples are

"A new command I give you: Love one another. As I have loved you, so you must love one another." (John 13:34)

"Go and make disciples of all nations." (Matthew 28:19)

"To the married I give this command (not I, but the Lord): A wife must not separate from her husband. But if she does, she must remain unmarried or else be reconciled to her husband. And a husband must not divorce his wife." (1 Corinthians 7:10-11)

Principles differ from direct commands. Principles are spiritual truths from the Bible that are found using accepted rules of interpretation. When interpreting a passage of Scripture, we observe the facts of the passage and then derive the meaning for the original audience, always being careful to note the historical, cultural, and literary context of the passage. Then we ask ourselves what application, if any, this interpretation has for us today, remembering that there is one interpretation, but many applications for a given passage of Scripture. This three-step method of Bible study— observation, interpretation, and application—will help us discover many biblical principles that we can apply in our daily lives.

An example of a biblical principle is found in Romans 14:23: "The man who has doubts is condemned if he eats, because his eating is not from faith; and everything that does not come from faith is sin." The context concerns whether or not a believer should eat meat or become a vegetarian. Paul declares that all food is clean and therefore may be eaten by Christians (verse 20). But in addition to considering the effect on others if we eat meat, we must also examine ourselves to see if we have doubts about it. If we do have doubts, it is better not to eat meat, for it would be sin for us to do so. The principle for us today is this: When facing practices in which our participation is morally dubious, we must examine ourselves to see if we have doubts about participating. If we have doubts, we should not proceed, for to do so would be sin for us.

Besides commands and principles, the Bible also contains numerous *promises* for believers. *Merriam-Webster's Collegiate Dictionary* defines a promise as a "declaration that gives the person to whom it is made a right to expect or to claim the performance or forbearance of a specified act." Thus, a worthy promise is a statement we can trust, one in which we can put our full confidence. But promises are only as good as the character and resources of the promise maker.

Suppose that today I were to promise to give you one million dollars tomorrow. No doubt you would be excited about the possibilities of spending or investing the money. However, you're in for a disappointment. I may have had the best intentions in making my promise, but unfortunately my resources are not adequate to fulfill it.

But praise God; His promises are different! A promise

from God is a pledge or declaration made by the living God. It gives us, as believers, the right to claim in our prayers His faithfulness to His pledge. We can expect that God will fulfill His promises because His perfect character and infinite resources back up what He has promised. He will be faithful to His Word. We can depend on it!

God gives promises that we might grow in Christlikeness and that we might live victorious lives above the current of sin in the world. Ask the Lord to help you become more proactive in pleading the promises in His Word.

Types of Promises

There are a couple of different ways of categorizing promises, but let us note first that all promises require faith for their fulfillment, for as Romans 4:16 reminds us, "The promise comes by faith." Faith is necessary in order to receive God's promises, but not a great amount of faith. What we need is faith in a great and faithful God. As we grow in our knowledge of God—His character and greatness—our faith will also grow.

One way to categorize the Bible's promises is to divide them into *general* promises and *specific* promises. General promises are given to many people and for all time. Key words in some general promises are "whoever," "he who," "believe," and "obey," indicating the conditions for the fulfillment of these promises. Some examples of general promises are

"Whoever believes in him [God's Son] shall not perish but have eternal life." (John 3:16)

"Whoever has my commands and obeys them . . . will be loved by my Father, and I too will love him and show myself to him." (John 14:21)

"Live by the Spirit, and you will not gratify the desires of the sinful nature." (Galatians 5:16)

"'Honor your father and mother'—which is the first commandment with a promise—'that it may go well with you and that you may enjoy long life on the earth.'" (Ephesians 6:2-3; see also Deuteronomy 5:16)

I can't tell you how precious my wife and I found God's general promises during the months rapidly approaching the delivery date of our first child, Michael. We lacked all of the necessities for a new baby. As struggling graduate students with little money, saving as much as possible to pay the anticipated doctor and hospital bills, we had no extra funds for those essential baby items. We were brand-new at this; we needed everything. What should we do?

As Dana and I prayed together about this, the Lord reminded us of His promise in Philippians 4:19: "My God will meet all your needs according to his glorious riches in Christ Jesus." We made a list of all the things that we needed—genuinely, desperately *needed*—for our new addition. Everything from two dozen diaper pins to a bassinet, from a changing table to rattles. We daily prayed and asked our heavenly Father to provide for us as He had promised. And one by one these items were given to us until everything on our list was provided. God cared not only for the physical provision for our child, but also for our confident peace of mind. Our faith took another step of growth through that experience.

Besides general promises, God sometimes gives us specific promises that relate to our unique situations and times. The Holy Spirit impresses these special passages of Scripture on our hearts and gives us an inner assurance that this is part of His special leading. The immediate context of the passage may seem unique to a biblical person in ancient times, but today's recipient hears God's voice speaking to his or her heart concerning his or her current situation.

Though such personal promises are a means by which God reveals and confirms His will to us, we must always remember that this is a very subjective process. "The heart is deceitful above all things," Jeremiah 17:9 tells us, and we are capable of reading into certain passages of Scripture what we want to see. We can deceive ourselves if we are not careful.

General and specific promises are given to believers for guidance and encouragement. Though general promises are many, specific promises are few. We should not expect to have specific promises given to us very often, and when we do find one, we must be certain that it is God speaking to us. A key is to have an attitude of expectancy as we approach the Scriptures, longing to meet with God and to hear His voice, expecting to fellowship with Him through His Word. Most of the time we will find encouragement and comfort from the general promises in the Word. But occasionally the Lord may also impress upon our hearts some passages of Scripture that will be very specific for our current situation or need, involving an interpretation that most people would not take from the passage. We are also to believe and act upon these special promises.

Another way to categorize the Bible's promises is to divide them into *conditional* and *unconditional* promises. Some promises are conditional upon our fulfilling certain acts of obedience before we will see God's fulfillment. Without our meeting these conditions, the promise will not be fulfilled. Abraham was given a great promise of blessing from the Lord, yet he still had to leave his home, extended family, and friends and go to a place that would later be shown to him. The great potential of the promise would have gone unrealized had he not acted upon it. The promises of God are ours as well, full of potential blessing and encouragement. Yet we sometimes have to act upon them if we are to experience the potential.

For example, in Galatians 5:16, the promise, "You will not gratify the desires of the sinful nature" is dependent on the condition that we "live by the Spirit." And the promise "that it may go well with you and that you may enjoy long life on the earth" will be fulfilled when we obey the associated command, "Honor your father and mother" (Ephesians 6:2-3; see also Deuteronomy 5:16).

In contrast, unconditional promises will be fulfilled for the believer in Jesus who simply accepts them by faith as being true. For example, the one who has placed genuine faith in Jesus need do nothing more in order to be assured of eternal life (John 3:16) or any of the spiritual blessings listed in Ephesians 1:3-14. That said, even though we are freely given these unconditional promises, we still must choose, by faith, whether or not to live in the full experience of their assurance and enjoyment. Pleading these promises in prayer is one way to enter into their fullest blessing.

Promises and Discerning God's Will

Knowing how to discern God's will for us and finding His path forward can be challenging. With so many options and competing voices, the cacophony can be distracting or confusing at best. How can we know His will for us?

Specific promises are helpful, but, because discerning such promises is a subjective process, this type of guidance should be used in conjunction with the five other means the Lord uses:

- *Clear commands and principles from the Word of God.* Since God is always truthful, no subjective guidance from Him will ever lead us in a way that would contradict His revealed Word (Psalm 119:105).
- *Inner conviction and peace from the Holy Spirit.* When we pray about our situation, God's Spirit, who dwells

within us, will confirm with our spirits that we are on the right path. This does not mean that we will have all the answers for our questions, but there will be quietness within our souls that He is leading us (Isaiah 30:21).

- *Wise counsel from mature believers.* In the abundance of counselors is much wisdom (Proverbs 15:22). Therefore, we seek a general consensus from those who are mature in the Lord, who want God's best for us.

- *Critical thinking.* I often write out pro-con lists when making a major decision. Dawson Trotman, the founder of The Navigators, said that "God gave you a lot of leading when He gave you a brain. So use it!" Proverbs 3:5-6 doesn't tell us not to *use* our understanding; it says not to *lean* on it—that is, don't place your total confidence in your ability to think or use logic alone for discovering God's will. His will for us can be counterintuitive or illogical from the world's perspective.

- *Providential circumstances.* The Lord can direct through open doors as well as closed doors. But we are not necessarily expected to walk through every open door. Our adversary can also open doors of opportunity to get us off track. Paul was directed by God on his second missionary journey when he ran into three closed doors, finally receiving a vision that directed him to Europe (Acts 16:6-10).

God wants us to know His will. He designed us to accomplish it. Thus He will direct us if we ask Him and use discernment to ensure it is His voice we're hearing, not just our own desires. As Romans 12:1-2 confirms, the key to knowing God's will is our willingness to obey it. God, being God, has no trouble communicating; He can easily cause all five of these guidance methods to align and point to a common pathway. The challenge is in following the path! For God's path requires faith and often sacrifice, and those can scare us.

I remember facing just such fear at a key turning point in my life. It was the fall of 1979, and I was two years into my veterinary medicine practice at a central Indiana equine clinic. For some time I had been wrestling with the idea of leaving the practice to join Navigator staff full time. We had been involved with a ministry to married couples at Purdue University for about seven years, and God seemed to be leading us into a full-time ministry position. As I thought through this decision, one of the nagging questions that persisted was how would I provide for my family? Or rather, how could God provide for my family? At that time we had two children, and I knew that joining The Navigators meant living by gift income. The Navigators, being a faith mission, do not guarantee a salary for their staff. All staff live by faith on the donations of interested friends and churches. Poverty—even a lack of the necessities of life—was a major concern as I considered this calling.

One morning in my devotional time I was studying and

meditating in the book of James. God spoke to my heart as I read James 2:5:

> Listen, my dear brothers: Has not God chosen those who are poor in the eyes of the world to be rich in faith and to inherit the kingdom he promised those who love him?

It was as if God was saying, "Tom, what's the worst that could possibly happen?"

Well, I thought, *we could become poor, not having enough money for what we need. But actually, James says that God has given the poor great faith; so in reality being poor would be a blessing rather than a burden. A lack of money would become an opportunity to grow in faith as we see God provide.*

From that day I began to pray over this passage, asking God to make me rich in faith as we stepped out from a regular salary and began to live by faith from gift income. The Lord used this passage, along with several others, to help confirm His will in leading me out of a career in veterinary medicine and into a career in missions. And I can now testify to God's faithfulness; He has increased our faith as well as provided very well for our family for the past thirty-six years.

The more we use the five means of guidance, the more confidence we can have that God is leading us. If, for instance, I had a specific promise and inner peace about something, yet godly counsel and circumstances were against it, it would be unwise to proceed. It may be that I have misinterpreted

God's leading, or it may simply be wrong timing. In either case, waiting would be the best solution. Time tends to clarify the uncertainties. Those people who press ahead in situations like these usually regret it afterward. As Proverbs 19:2 reminds us,

> It is not good to have zeal without knowledge,
> nor to be hasty and miss the way.

Or, said another way, "There are good decisions and fast decisions, but few good, fast decisions." Impatience is often a sign of spiritual immaturity.

It is not difficult for God, being sovereign and omnipotent, to lead us, and He knows our difficulties in discerning His will. We have Jesus' promise that the Holy Spirit, who lives within us, will guide us (John 16:13; Psalm 32:8). A sincere believer, who is truly seeking God's will, can be certain of being led by Him.

FOR THOUGHT AND DISCUSSION

Think of a scriptural promise you would like God to fulfill in your life. Is it a general promise, or is it specific to you? Is it conditional or unconditional for you as a believer in Christ?

In light of your answers, what is your next step in this journey of faith as you trust Him and His promises?

2

A THEOLOGY OF PROMISES

God is not a man, that he should lie,
   nor a son of man, that he should change his mind.
NUMBERS 23:19

And this is what he promised us—even eternal life.
I JOHN 2:25

SOME TIME AGO I was studying some of the bolder prayers of the Bible—for example, Jabez asking for the blessing of God (1 Chronicles 4:9-10) or Moses asking to see God's glory (Exodus 33:18). I noted that these bold, outlandish, seemingly selfish requests were granted by God. After finishing the study and reflecting upon possible applications for my own life, I asked this question: "What would be the boldest request I could personally make of God?"

I remembered that God makes covenants with us, that He binds Himself in solemn covenants of promise and delights in fulfilling His promises. In particular, I recalled the Lord's covenant promise to Abraham:

> I will make you into a great nation
>   and I will bless you;
> I will make your name great,
>   and you will be a blessing.
> I will bless those who bless you,
>   and whoever curses you I will curse;
> and all peoples on earth
>   will be blessed through you.
>   (Genesis 12:2-3; see also 17:7; 26:3-5; 28:13-15)

God promised to bless all the nations through Abraham and his descendants, and that promise was renewed again through the messianic prophecy in Isaiah 49:6:

> I will also make you a light for the Gentiles,
>   that you may bring my salvation to the ends of the
>   earth.

The apostle Paul quoted this text to a hostile crowd in Pisidian Antioch (Acts 13:47), demonstrating that this Abrahamic covenant is still in force today; it applies to those under the New Covenant, Abraham's spiritual offspring.

After some more reflection, I decided that the most I could ask God for would be the entire world! But how would I be able to see or measure His answer?

I began to ask the Lord to bless me and make me a blessing to the nations, just as He had blessed Abraham. To make it measurable and to focus my prayers, I asked the Lord to allow me the privilege of naming men and women on every continent of the world whom I've personally discipled or influenced deeply. Isaiah 49:6 became one of my life promises; I've gone back to it over and over again as I keep on asking God for the world. After several decades, I can now name people on four of the seven continents. The one I can't wait to see God answer will be Antarctica!

In Christ . . .

Because we are in Christ, God promises to be everything for us. J. I. Packer says this concerning the Promiser:

> Biblical religion has the form of a covenant relation with God. The first occasion on which the terms of the relation were made plain was when God showed Himself to Abraham as *El Shaddai* (God Almighty, God All-sufficient) and formally gave him the covenant promise, "to be a God unto thee" (Gen. 17:1ff, 7). All Christians inherit this promise through faith in Christ, as Paul argues in Galatians 3:15ff (note verse 29). What does it mean? It is in truth a pantechnicon promise: it contains everything. "This is the first and fundamental promise," declared Sibbes, the Puritan, "indeed, it is the life and soul of all the promises" (*Works* VI, 8).[1]

The promise-making God we have come to know through receiving Jesus Christ as our Savior can be trusted to keep His promises. His character backs up His promises. He is a God of truth; He cannot lie (Numbers 23:19). Theologian Henry Thiessen writes that God's faithfulness

> leads him to fulfill all his promises, whether expressed in words or implied in the constitution he has given us (Deut. 7:9; Isa. 25:1). That God is faithful to himself (2 Tim. 2:13), to his Word (Heb. 11:11), and to his people (1 Cor. 1:9; 10:13; 1 Thes. 5:24; 2 Thes. 3:3) is an abiding source of encouragement and strength for the believer.[2]

We have numerous witnesses in Scripture who testified that God fulfills His promises. Joshua (21:45), David (Psalm 145:13), Solomon (1 Kings 8:20,24,56), Nehemiah (9:7-8), and Paul (Acts 13:32-33) all state emphatically that God will not allow one of His promises to fail; all will be fulfilled. When God says something once, it is important. But if He repeats Himself, we had better take notice! Multiple Bible writers and characters, under the inspiration of the Holy Spirit, affirm the faithfulness of God to all His promises.

When we put our trust in Jesus Christ as our personal Savior and Lord, we are promised the forgiveness of our sin (1 John 1:9), our old nature is crucified with Christ (Romans 6:6), and we are given the Holy Spirit to live within us (Romans 8:10; 1 Corinthians 6:19), helping us live the life God desires (Romans 8:11; Galatians 5:16). We are placed into Christ and adopted as children of God (John

1:12; Romans 8:15-17), and as such we have access to all the promises of God in Christ (Galatians 3:9,29; 4:7). Paul confirms in 2 Corinthians 1:20-22 that God puts His personal guarantee on His Word to us:

> No matter how many promises God has made, they are "Yes" in Christ. And so through him the "Amen" is spoken by us to the glory of God. Now it is God who makes both us and you stand firm in Christ. He anointed us, set his seal of ownership on us, and put his Spirit in our hearts as a deposit, guaranteeing what is to come.

John MacArthur, commenting on the many "spiritual blessings" promised to us in Ephesians 1:3-14, writes,

> Our every conceivable need is met by God's gracious provision in accordance with His divine promises. We are promised peace, love, grace, wisdom, eternal life, joy, victory, strength, guidance, power, mercy, forgiveness, righteousness, truth, fellowship with God, spiritual discernment, heaven, eternal riches, glory—those and every other good thing that comes from God.[3]

Rightly Handling the Word

Though we have the right to plead all the promises of God because we are in Christ, we must be careful to exercise the rules of good historical-grammatical interpretation when applying these passages to ourselves—especially promises found in the Old Testament. We must first make appropriate *observations* of the text as we study the original context of the passage. Next we must seek to *interpret* the text, discerning its meaning for the original audience and determining in what ways the passage's truths can be carried over into our current situation. Lastly, we must bridge the gap back to our present situation and *apply* the truths in the text to our lives.

During this application step, when seeking to apply a passage to our current day and time, we need to discern whether it is a general promise given to all or a specific promise. If it is a general promise we are seeking to apply, then we can simply substitute our names into the text, personalizing it for ourselves. But if it is a specific promise limited to a specific person, time, or situation, we need to be careful about applying the text to ourselves. We must be certain that it is God speaking to us through the passage and not we ourselves who are reading our own desires into the text. Remembering that specific promises are only one means by which God leads us and also remembering our own weaknesses, we should recognize the other means that God uses to guide us and not weigh this subjective evidence too heavily. If this leading is from God, then He will confirm it with other more objective means, such as counsel from mature believers and objective reasoning.

Following is an example—slightly adapted from Warren

Myers,[4] author of several books on prayer—of properly handling the text of Isaiah 45:1-3 and praying its promises:

> This is what the LORD says to his anointed,
>   to Cyrus, whose right hand I take hold of
> to subdue nations before him
>   and to strip kings of their armor,
> to open doors before him
>   so that gates will not be shut:
> I will go before you
>   and will level the mountains;
> I will break down gates of bronze
>   and cut through bars of iron.
> I will give you the treasures of darkness,
>   riches stored in secret places,
> so that you may know that I am the LORD,
>   the God of Israel, who summons you by name.

1. *Observation:* This promise was given to Cyrus and refers to the conquering of nations. Cyrus was used as God's instrument to return Israel to the land after the captivity.
2. *Interpretation:* It shows God's willingness and power to work for and with His chosen vessels, overcoming enemies and hindrances, in order to accomplish His purposes for His people. This promise is also in line with Jesus' promise in Mark 11:22-24.

   Today God calls us not to conquer nations but

people for Him. The chief enemy is not kings but Satan, who often has human cooperation. The usual hindrances are attitudes, thoughts, values, or situations that need His transforming touch.

3. *Application:* Even as God did these things for Cyrus, I believe He wants to do them in our family and ministry, and I am believing Him to do this in the life of _____ who is resisting His will, and in my ministry at _____.[5]

Herbert Lockyer says this concerning the application of the Bible to our present situation:

It is so essential to remember . . . the rule, so often lost sight of: While all the Bible was written for us, not all of it was written to us. Promises made to particular persons, and in cases and for reasons that equally concern other saints, are yet applicable to the comfort of all, and may be pleaded with faith and prayer. Paul thus writes—"For everything that was written in the past was written to teach us, so that through endurance and the encouragement of the Scriptures we might have hope" (Romans 15:4).[6]

Testing the Promises

The first time I can remember pleading a promise in prayer (other than for my salvation), we were living in married student housing on the campus of Purdue University. I was a third-year veterinary medical student, and Dana was pregnant with our first child. Living in a one-bedroom apartment, we needed to make room for the new member of our family. A couple of months before the delivery date I contacted the housing authority and asked them to remove the university's furniture. In addition to removing a bed and bureau, they also took our one bookcase.

As you might imagine, the bookcase was a necessary piece of furniture for a student. Because we were saving every penny to pay for the baby, we decided to commit our need to the Lord. I had just memorized Psalm 37:4:

> Delight yourself in the LORD
> and he will give you the desires of your heart.

This is a conditional promise—that is, if we meet the conditions stated, then God will do as He promised. As we talked about it, it seemed that we were, to the best of our abilities, seeking to put the Lord first in all areas of our life; in other words, we were delighting in Him. Thus we could expectantly plead our heart's desire for a bookcase. After careful consideration we prayed over the general promise in Philippians 4:19: "My God will meet all your needs according to his glorious riches in Christ Jesus," and we asked God to meet this need of ours. I told the Lord my heart's desire was a bookcase made from one-by-twelve-inch pine boards, stained walnut, and separated with cement blocks.

We began to pray to this end, covenanting not to tell anyone other than God. With the due date fast approaching, we saw no bookcase, and I was getting a little discouraged and tired of reminding the Lord about this need. Then one night we were returning to our apartment after attending a Bible study when we met a neighbor in the parking lot. He mentioned that he had just graduated and would be moving soon to begin work. He was getting rid of some of their things, and he wanted to know if we needed a bookcase.

Trying to maintain my excitement, I replied that as a matter of fact we might be interested. He escorted me into his apartment where he showed me his bookcase. Made from one-by-twelve-inch pine boards, stained walnut, and separated by cement blocks!

"It's yours if you want it," he said.

"Thanks!" I said. I went home rejoicing that the Lord had answered, and I praised Him for His faithfulness.

God wants dependent, not independent, children. He wants us to be ever more reliant upon Him. Thus He allows times of testing in our lives that will give us opportunities to depend more upon Him and His Word, that He might prove His faithfulness. It is through these times of testing that we grow in maturity and faith and learn more about the character of God. That is why James can say, "Consider it pure joy, my brothers, whenever you face trials of many kinds, because you know that the testing of your faith develops perseverance. Perseverance must finish its work so that you may be mature and complete, not lacking anything" (1:2-4). These testings are for our benefit.

A story is told about the building of a great suspension bridge across a raging river. The first step for the builders was to fly a kite across the falls. Once the kite had landed on the opposite side of the river, the string was secured. To this one string was tied a heavier cord, which was then pulled across the turbulent waters, and to that one another was added, which was heavier yet. And so it went, line added to line until a steel cable was stretched across the river. Additional cables were also added until at last the great bridge was completed. None would have dreamed from looking at the completed bridge that the construction had begun with the flying of a kite.

And so it is in the development of our faith. Those of great faith do not get there except by adding trial upon trial, testing the promises of God over and over again. With each testing comes another opportunity to see the Lord demonstrate His ability to us. And each time we experience His answers, as we plead His promises, we add a heavier cord of faith to our lives. Unfortunately, the faith of many believers is still in the kite-flying stage, when we should be stringing steel cables of faith across the turbulent waters of the trials we face in life.

The Lord, knowing our weakness and quickness to succumb to pressure brought on by trials, has filled the Bible with a multitude of promises—some have counted as many as seven thousand!—to strengthen us in our times of doubt.

Some of the promises that I return to over and over again for strength and encouragement are these:

> Call upon me in the day of trouble;
>   I will deliver you, and you will honor me.
> (Psalm 50:15)

> Do not fear, for I am with you;
>   do not be dismayed, for I am your God.
> I will strengthen you and help you;
>   I will uphold you with my righteous right hand.
> (Isaiah 41:10)

> A bruised reed he will not break,
> and a smoldering wick he will not snuff out.
> (Isaiah 42:3)

> Ah, Sovereign LORD, you have made the heavens and the earth by your great power and outstretched arm. Nothing is too hard for you.
> (Jeremiah 32:17)

> Nothing is impossible with God.
> (Luke 1:37)

With these promises and many more, the Lord is encouraging us to "cast all [our] anxiety on him" (1 Peter 5:7). We must learn to rest in Him and His promises, letting Him carry the burden of our trials. He has proven and will always prove Himself worthy of our trust.

For Thought and Discussion

In a few sentences, use your own words to summarize the Bible's most important teachings about God's promises. Describe what your life would be like if you believed these truths and acted upon them with 100-percent conviction.

3

PEOPLE WHO HAVE PRAYED
THE PROMISES

God's promises are never broken by leaning upon them.
HOWARD HENDRICKS

HISTORY IS FULL of ordinary people who have taken God at His word and seen Him do extraordinary things in and through them. They are not special in that they had extraordinary faith. Their faith was ordinary, but it grew as they trusted the promises of God and saw God answer prayer. They were normal people who lived supernormal lives because they prayed the promises of God.

Starting as far back as the 1500s, Martin Luther was a man who prayed the promises of God. He took a very personal approach to the Scriptures, asserting that "the correct way of reading the Bible is through the right use of the personal pronouns: 'Every promise of God is made to me.'"[1]

Charles H. Spurgeon, the renowned English preacher of the nineteenth century, was fond of praying over the promises of the Bible. In the preface to one of his works, Spurgeon wrote,

> The sight of the promises themselves is good for the eyes of faith; the more we study the words of grace, the more grace we shall derive from the words. To the cheering Scriptures I have added testimonies of my own, the fruit of trial and experience. I believe the promises of God, but many of them I have personally tried and proved.[2]

D. L. Moody, the famous nineteenth-century evangelist and preacher, regularly prayed the promises of God's Word in prayer and encouraged others to do the same. Part of his evangelistic crusade program would routinely involve "a promise meeting, which consisted of testimonies on the part of believers to the fulfillment of promises in their own experiences."[3]

When organizing one particular convocation for prayer, Moody wrote in the invitation,

> A gathering is hereby called to meet in Northfield, Mass., from September 1st to 10th inclusive, the object of which is not so much to study the Bible (though the Scriptures will be searched daily for instruction and promises) as for solemn self-consecration, for pleading God's promises, and

waiting upon Him for a fresh anointment of power from on high.[4]

Moody urged believers always to carry a Bible or a New Testament, carefully marking God's promises, among other key texts.[5] His conviction concerning the promises of God can be summarized in his own words:

> Take the promises of God. Let a man feed for a month on the promises of God, and he will not talk about how poor he is. You hear people say, "Oh, my leanness! How lean I am!" It is not their leanness, it is their laziness. If you would only read from Genesis to Revelation and see all the promises made by God to Abraham, to Isaac, to Jacob, to the Jews and to the Gentiles, and to all His people everywhere—if you would spend a month feeding on the precious promises of God—you wouldn't be going about complaining how poor you are. You would lift up your head and proclaim the riches of His Grace, because you couldn't help doing it![6]

During the course of his influential career in the late 1800s and early 1900s, Dr. R. A. Torrey served as a local pastor, a traveling evangelist, superintendent of Moody Bible Institute, and dean of the Bible Institute of Los Angeles. According to him, one of the most important keys to effective prayer was "to study the Word of God to find what God's will is as revealed there in the promises, and then simply to take these promises and spread them out in prayer before God with the absolutely unwavering expectation that He will do what He has promised in His Word."[7]

J. O. Fraser was a famous twentieth-century missionary to the Lisu people of southwest China. During his lifetime he saw many Lisu trust Christ as a result of his prayers and the prayers of those who interceded for his ministry. He offered a challenging but tempered thought on our topic:

> We are often exhorted, and with reason, to ask great things of God. Yet there is a balance in all things, and we may go too far in this direction. It is possible to bite off, in prayer, more than we can chew. . . . Over-strained faith is not pure faith; there is a mixture of the carnal element in it. . . .
>
> I have definitely asked the Lord for several hundred families of Lisu believers. There are upward of two thousand Lisu families in the Tantsah district. It might be said, "Why do you not ask for a thousand?" I answer quite frankly, "Because I have not faith for a thousand." I believe the Lord has given me faith for more than one hundred families, but not for a thousand. So I accept the limits the Lord, I believe, has given me. Perhaps God will give me a thousand; perhaps He will lead me to commit myself to this definite prayer of faith later on. This is in accordance with Ephesians 3:20: 'above all that

we ask or think.' But we must not overload faith; we must be sane and practical. Let us not claim too little in faith, but let us not claim too much either."[8]

Robert A. Jaffray, Christian and Missionary Alliance missionary pioneer who served in China and Indochina and opened their work in Indonesia, was another who learned the habit of praying the promises of God. "He literally soaked his heart in the Word of God," A. W. Tozer wrote of Jaffray. "He did not 'study' it, he devoured it, he dug himself into it, he transferred its stories and promises to himself and his work with as much assurance as if the whole Bible had been written for him alone."[9]

The nineteenth century has been described as the Great Century of Missions, and Hudson Taylor, the founder of China Inland Mission (today known as Overseas Missionary Fellowship International), was one of the most influential missionaries of that period. His example has continued to motivate and challenge many, including me, in their walk with God. When describing Taylor, his biographers said, "Above all, he put to the test the promises of God, and proved it possible to live a consistent spiritual life on the highest plane."[10] Taylor was raised in a family that regularly prayed over the promises of the Scriptures. "Brought up in such a circle," Taylor wrote, "and saved under such circumstances, it was perhaps natural that from the very commencement of my Christian life I was led to feel that the promises of the Bible are very real, and that prayer is in sober fact transacting business with God, whether on one's own behalf or on behalf of those for whom one seeks His blessing."[11]

As a young and inexperienced missionary, Taylor encountered severe difficulties after his arrival in China. He wrote home, "I am so apt, like Peter, to take my eyes off the One to be trusted and look at the winds and waves. . . . Oh for more stability! The reading of the Word and meditation on the promises have been increasingly precious to me of late."[12]

It was his belief that by prayer alone God would supply all his needs and those of the mission. It was enough to tell God only; He would move the hearts of men to meet their needs. Later in life, when Taylor was back in England, a visitor to the mission headquarters said,

> One day, when we had had a small breakfast and
> there was scarcely anything for dinner, I was thrilled
> to hear [Mr. Taylor] singing the children's hymn:
> "Jesus loves me, this I know, For the Bible tells me
> so." Then he called us together to praise the Lord
> for His changeless love, to tell our needs and claim
> the promises. And before the day was over we were
> rejoicing in His gracious answers.[13]

And in April 1874, when the balance in the mission's bank account was down to twenty-five cents, he wrote his wife this note, "We have this—and all the promises of God."[14] Summarizing his attitude towards the promises of God he wrote, "The living God still lives, and the living Word is a living Word, and we may depend upon it. We may hang upon any word God ever spoke or caused by His Holy Spirit to be written."[15]

George Mueller was another nineteenth-century man of God who trusted the Lord alone to supply for his ministry to orphans and saw many wonderful answers to prayer. Toward the end of his life he wrote,

> When I first began to allow God to deal with me, relying on Him, taking Him at His Word, and set out fifty years ago simply relying on Him for myself, family, taxes, traveling expenses and every other need, I rested on the simple promises I found in the sixth chapter of Matthew [Matthew 6:25-33]. I believed the Word; I rested on it and practiced it. I took God at His Word . . . I put my reliance in the God who has promised, and He has acted according to His Word.[16]

The Navigators' Rich Heritage

As a young man, Dawson Trotman, founder of The Navigators, was deeply influenced by the biographies of George Mueller and Hudson Taylor. Their deep commitment to prayer and simple trust in God challenged him to imitate their example.

Trotman began to devote extended time to prayer and study of God's Word. His biographer wrote,

Dawson felt free to take personally a promise or command intended for one of another era in God's timetable. . . . As he kept his prayer appointments in the hills, Dawson began to look for promises God would give to him. His faith in the Word was being strengthened, and there was growing reality in his relationship with the God who spoke and it was done, who commanded and it stood fast. . . .[17]

With due respect to dispensationalists, he still did not feel Scripture should be apportioned to certain peoples for certain times exclusively. In the margin above Jeremiah he wrote, "Is it possible that God wrote this whole Book to one small people, or did He, knowing the end from the beginning, write to others herein." And beside Isaiah 58:12 he wrote, "Given many times when praying about my life work." Why should Christians who claim God's promise of peace from Isaiah 26:3 or forgiveness of sin from Isaiah 1:18 consider the promise in Isaiah 58:12 off limits? Even Isaiah 58:11, "And the Lord shall guide thee continually," was commonly claimed and quoted. Telling later of God's promises to him from Isaiah for his life work, he explained with a light touch, "Some say the Book of Isaiah is for the Jews. Well it's full of promises, and as I looked around, I didn't see the Jews claiming them— somebody should be using them!"[18]

Lorne Sanny, former international director of The Navigators once remarked to Trotman, "You impress me as one who feels he is a man of destiny, one destined to be used of God."

"I don't think that's the case," Trotman replied, "but I know this. God has given me some promises that I know He will fulfill."[19]

Trotman's firm convictions concerning prayer and God's promises deeply influenced Sanny and cemented the foundation of The Navigators:

It was his prayer life that recruited me to The Navigators. . . . During those prayer times I learned about appropriating the promises of God. Years later in our *Fundamentals of the Ministry* (page 30), Jim Petersen wrote, 'The prayer of faith appropriates His promises. The response of faith obeys His commands.' That is profoundly true. To me, it is the reason there is a Navigator ministry today.[20]

Sanny himself contributed, through faith, to The Navigators' heritage. At age forty, after five years as Navigators president, in the midst of a midlife crisis he felt the need for "a fresh word from God." He took two and a half months away from his ministry responsibilities. Later, in a staff prayer letter, he confided:

I asked the Lord to call me by name, not knowing how He would do that. But I wanted to know God was speaking to me. . . .

One day I was meditating on the sufferings of the Savior in Isaiah 53. I told the Lord how barren I was in winning the lost. I said, "Lord, I am the most barren person in The Navigators." Then I began reading the next chapter. It began, "Sing, O barren." It was as though the Lord said, *Okay, you asked Me to call you by name, you called yourself "Barren," we will use that one.* Then the Lord began to assure me that Isaiah 54:1-3 was for me.

Key words in that passage—'sing . . . enlarge . . . let them . . . lengthen . . . strengthen . . . nations'— became operative words for me and others over the next twenty-five years. The Lord seemed to be saying, *Go for it, the whole world, every nation.*

God had given Daws Isaiah 43:4-7 in the early days, and He renewed it to me during this time. Nineteen years later the 1980 International Leadership Conference would bring "sons and daughters" from east, west, north, and south. What was a first in 1980 has become a regular happening throughout the world as Navigators are going from everywhere to everywhere, lengthening the cords and strengthening the stakes. We now have ministries in more than eighty countries. Isaiah 54:1-3 and Isaiah 43:4-7 are steel threads in the fabric of the Navigator ministry today.[21]

Praying over the promises of God will lead one to see and experience the faithfulness of God.

Not Just for "Giants"

I often speak at conferences on the subject of faith and the promises of God. At the conclusion of a message on praying specifically over God's general promises of provision (for example, Philippians 4:19) and God's generosity in promising to give us the desires of our hearts (for example, Psalm 37:4), I ask the audience to make an "Impossible List"—needs and desires they would like to see God answer in the next six months. I remind them that they have access to unlimited resources and power through Christ; nothing is impossible with Him (Luke 1:37)!

This Impossible List is a prayer exercise designed to build one's "faith muscle" through praying specifically and seeing God answer specifically. It's important to start with a request that is tangible and measurable, so that we know when He answers. There is nothing sacred in the six-month duration. It's long enough for larger issues to be addressed and yet not so long as to wear out the pray-er. It creates a limited-focus prayer effort that's long enough to build good prayer habits.

At one conference a student placed at the top of her Impossible List the salvation of her father. She had become a Christian as a student and always longed for her parents to come to faith in Christ. Her mother had recently converted, but her ability to communicate with her father was challenging at best.

After the meeting ended, she called home to let her parents know of her safe arrival at the conference. Her father answered the phone. After she had shared that all was well, her dad inquired about the first night's meeting. She explained about her Impossible List, and he asked what she had put on her list.

"Well, Dad," she answered hesitantly, "the very first thing on my list is that you would come to know Jesus as your personal Savior."

There was a long pause, and then her father said, "You know, I've been thinking a lot about that subject recently. I've got a lot of questions."

That led to a long conversation in which this daughter was able to lead her father to faith in Christ on the phone that night! The next morning at breakfast she was so excited to be able to share with me that the number one item on her list had already been answered.

At another conference I again asked the audience to make out their six-month Impossible Lists. I routinely ask husbands and wives to make individual lists and then share the contents with each other. When comparing their lists, one couple had both written that their heart's desire was that God would give them twins.

A little over a year later I once again crossed paths with this couple. They were now the parents of twin girls!

Considering all of the faithful prayer warriors throughout the world, in all of history—people "great" and "small," well-known and completely unknown—we've examined only a tiny number of examples. Yet we can see that God's people have demonstrated His faithfulness to His promises throughout history. He is the same yesterday, today, and forever (Hebrews 13:8), and therefore we have the same opportunity to try and prove His promises. If we are willing, we can see Him do great and wonderful things, just as those who have gone before us.

We can and we will, as we rest in faith on His promises.

For Thought and Discussion

As a follower of Jesus, you no doubt desire to pray God's promises and thereby see extraordinary results in your life. Consider the examples of people in this chapter, and choose one attitude or habit that you want to cultivate in order to live an extraordinary life of faith. How, in practical terms, can you do this?

4

HOW TO PLEAD A PROMISE

The man took Jesus at his word and departed.

JOHN 4:50

"And now, LORD God, keep forever the promise you have made concerning your servant and his house. Do as you promised."

2 SAMUEL 7:25

Then they believed his promises and sang his praise.

PSALM 106:12

GOD HAD GIVEN ME A HEART for missions and for working among the poor. Isaiah 49:6 was one of the personal promises that God used to guide me into a career in helping bring the gospel "to the ends of the earth." After completing our staff training at Purdue University, we accepted an opportunity to serve in a student ministry with The Navigators in Indonesia.

With this opportunity came a sense of personal calling to the work there, and we busied ourselves looking at *National Geographic* articles with lots of pictures, trying to imagine what living there would be like. (Yes, this was before the Internet.) We moved to Chicago to wait for our visa and began to work on the details of moving our family of five to the other side of the world. We had been told to anticipate the visa taking six months to obtain. God continued to provide a house with a month-to-month lease and a new home church with many new friends and ministry partners.

But the visa was harder to obtain than we had been led to believe. We waited and waited with no progress in sight. Was I the reason for the delay? I searched my soul, confessing all known sin, keeping short accounts with God. But still no visa was granted.

Psalm 50:15 became an anchor for me while we waited:

> Call upon me in the day of trouble;
> I will deliver you, and you will honor me.

We prayed and reminded God of His promise to deliver us in this day of trouble, reminding Him of our situation, and pleading with Him for a visa for Indonesia. Months and years passed, but still no visa. I continually reviewed my promises and God's direction for us in prayer. But still no answer.

Friends and supporters began to ask, "Are you sure that God is leading you to Indonesia? With such a long delay, He must be saying no."

Each time I would get alone with God and once again pour out my heart, giving back to Him our lives and asking Him for an answer—any answer. Should we continue to wait, or should we consider another destination? Yes, I know. Hebrews 10:36 reminds us, "You need to persevere so that when you have done the will of God, you will receive what he has promised." Oh, but waiting is so, so hard!

Jacob

Jacob was no stranger to waiting. He had to work fourteen long years for the hand of Rachel. He waited at least that long to receive the fulfillment of God's promise to prosper him and his offspring (Genesis 28:13-15; renewed in 31:3,13). He was also willing to humbly remind God of His promise.

Jacob was preparing to meet Esau after a decade and a half of separation, not knowing whether he would be loved or hated. Genesis 32:7 says that he was in "fear and distress" as he brought his request to the Lord in prayer. Following a pattern that we're about to see is quite common among the godly; Jacob confessed his unworthiness and reviewed his current situation (verses 9-10). Then he reminded the Lord of His promise to bless and prosper him, asking specifically that he be delivered from the hand of his brother (verses 11-12).

Commenting on these verses, Norval Hadley of International Intercessors draws lines between verses 9 and 12.

> Jacob reminded God that He had promised, "I
> will prosper you." Have you noticed how often
> Bible prayers seem to be saying to God, "You must
> answer my prayer, because You promised. . . . Don't
> embarrass Yourself by failing to keep Your word.
> Bring glory to Yourself by doing what You said

You would do." That sounds a bit bold to us, but Hebrews 4:16 says we are to come boldly.[1]

Moses

Skip ahead a few hundred years, past the Egyptian sojourn and the Exodus. Here at Mt. Sinai we encounter God, enraged with Israel for the nation's disobedience in worshiping the golden calf—so angry in fact that He was considering destroying them all and from the descendants of Moses himself making a great nation (Exodus 32:9-10). And God was well within His rights under His own covenant with Israel.

But Moses made a specific request to the Lord: "Turn from your fierce anger; relent and do not bring disaster on your people" (verse 12). He reminded the Lord of His promises to Abraham, Isaac, and Israel (Jacob) to bless them and their offspring forever, and as Moses had requested, the Lord at last did relent of His intention to destroy Israel (verses 13-14). Because of the promise-invoking prayer of one man, the Lord Almighty spared millions.

David

Moses died, Joshua conquered the Promised Land, and the period of the judges gave way to the kingdom era. A man after God's heart took the throne, and we find this man, David, praying the promise of kingship for him and his descendants. Second Samuel 7:1-17 records the giving of the promise through the prophet Nathan; in verses 18-29 we see David's response.

David began his prayer with an attitude of humility and reverence for God, confessing his unworthiness of the Lord's blessing (verses 18-21). He reviewed with God the nation's status and praised the Lord for several of His character qualities (verses 22-24). Then David asked the Lord to "do as you promised" (verse 25). We can be sure this was only the first of many times that King David and his successors made specific requests based on the unbreakable promise that God had given David—a promise that would ultimately be fulfilled in the person of Jesus.

Daniel

Several hundred more years passed, and God's chosen people entered one of the darkest chapters of their history. The kingdom was divided, and first the North (Israel) and then the South (Judah) so grievously violated God's covenant that He used foreign nations to conquer them and carry them off into exile. During Judah's final days, God spoke through the prophet Jeremiah, foretelling His impending punishment for their disobedience. However, God also left His people with a note of hope—a promise that after seventy years of exile He would restore them to their land (Jeremiah 25:11-12; 29:10-14).

Daniel was a youth when Judah was conquered, and

he was carried away into captivity along with many other Jews. Having been in Babylon for approximately fifty years, he came across the promises to Jeremiah stating that the captivity would last only seventy years (Daniel 9:1-19). According to verse 3, Daniel "turned to the Lord God and pleaded with him in prayer and petition, in fasting, and in sackcloth and ashes." The NIV's choice of the English word *pleaded* here is especially apt, as it translates a Hebrew word that also conveys twofold meaning. The word can mean "to seek" or even "to beg"—this is the aspect reflected in Daniel's attitude of humility before the Lord—but it can also mean "to require," an aspect that comes through in the boldness with which Daniel make his requests, albeit from a prone position.

We, too, must bring this twofold attitude as we pray over the promises. We come before our Creator and Lord in reverence, awe, and holy fear; yet we come with confidence, knowing that as His sons and daughters we are gladly welcomed into audience with the King. Our confidence and boldness is especially appropriate when pleading God's promises; for then we know that God's own authority and character stand behind our requests.

Daniel began his prayer with a confession of his own sins and the sins and rebellion of his people. He acknowledged that the Lord was righteous in bringing this judgment of captivity upon them (verse 7). Then, in verses 8-14, Daniel reviewed with God the situation in which he and his fellow Jews then found themselves. In doing so he also reminded the Lord of His character—of His mercy and forgiveness in addition to His righteousness and justice. And finally, Daniel made his request based on God's promise through Jeremiah (verses 15-19). He asked specifically that the Lord would turn away His anger (verse 16) and would look with favor on the city of Jerusalem and the desolate sanctuary (verses 16-17). Daniel never dictated to God how He was to answer the request; but he did courageously plead God's merciful character as the basis for fulfillment of His promise.

God answered Daniel's request as He had promised. But He did so in His time.

Nehemiah

Some decades later, Nehemiah was part of the Lord's answer to Daniel's prayer.

Ezra had already led many Jews back to their homeland. He had led the rebuilding of the temple and the reimplementation of Mosaic Law. But many Jews still lived in exile in Persia—then the new world power—and the walls of Jerusalem still lay in disrepair. Nehemiah received some visitors from Jerusalem, and their dismal report of the city's condition moved Nehemiah's heart to pray (Nehemiah 1:1-11).

Nehemiah began his prayer and fasting as did Daniel and many before him—that is, by noting the character of God and confessing his sins and the sins of his people (verses 4-7). He then reminded the Lord of His promise—this time given through Moses (for example, Deuteronomy 4:25-31)—to gather the Israelites after He had scattered them (verses 8-9). Next he made his specific request for favor in the presence of the king of Persia (verse 11), as he was about to ask for permission to return to Jerusalem and rebuild the walls. God granted his request, and Nehemiah returned and accomplished the task.

Praying like Our Forefathers

By now I suspect you see the pattern for praying over a promise. Let me sum it up.

First, we come with a twofold attitude of both abject humility and courageous expectancy. We don't dictate to God, even when claiming His promises. But we do come boldly, reverentially, before His throne.

Second, we acknowledge before God our sinfulness and confess our sins as the Holy Spirit brings them to remembrance. We must not deceive ourselves into thinking that the Lord will honor our requests if we harbor unconfessed sin in our lives or if we are living in a condition of disobedience to His revealed will in the Bible.

Third, we bring before the Lord our concerns and the details of the situation. It is not that the omniscient Lord needs more information; rather, in doing this, our thoughts clarify and the Lord can help us better understand and gain perspective on our current situation.

Fourth, it is good to remind the Lord of certain related character qualities, not only pleading that He act in keeping with His character, but also asking Him to build these into our lives during this testing of our faith.

And fifth, when we pray a promise, we also make our specific request based on the promises in the Word. Though we do make specific requests, we again must yield to the Lord the right to answer in His way and in His time. He alone can see all things; He knows what circumstances and timing are best for us. Having a demanding spirit regarding either the means or the time of God's answer is a sign of spiritual immaturity. As someone has said, "God is never in a hurry, but He is always on time."

You will find it very helpful if you memorize the verses you are claiming in prayer. This will enable you to meditate on the Word while you go about your daily routine. Also, if you ever find yourself anxious about the promise's fulfillment, you can stop and pray through the promise in your mind, again asking the Lord to do as He has promised. I personally keep a written record of the promises I have prayed and how God has answered. I regularly review this list of past pleas and answers when facing a present testing of my faith. It's a tremendous source of encouragement.

In his *Faith's Checkbook*, a collection of God's promises for daily use, Charles Spurgeon wrote this about how to pray a promise:

A promise of God may very instructively be
compared to a check payable to order. It is given to
the believer with the view of bestowing upon him

some good thing. It is not meant that he should read it over comfortably, and then have done with it. No, he is to treat the promise as a reality, as a man treats a check. He is to take the promise, and endorse it with his own name, by personally receiving it as true. He is by faith to accept it as his own. He sets to his seal that God is true, and true as to this particular word of promise. He goes further and believes that he has the blessing in having the sure promise of it, and therefore he puts his name to it to testify to the receipt of the blessing.

This done, he must believingly present the promise to the Lord, as a man presents a check at the counter of the bank. He must plead it by prayer, expecting to have it fulfilled.[2]

Waiting and Winning

So, as my burden for Indonesia continued, I prayed. And I believed. And I pleaded. And I expected.

I humbled myself, coming to God in reverential boldness.

I confessed my sins, spelling out my situation before God.

I pleaded His character qualities and His promises as the basis for letting us go to Indonesia.

And God took His perfect time. But He never forgot His promises.

And finally, after three years of waiting, our visa was granted.

Victory? Absolutely. But now we faced a radically differ-ent challenge. At this point we had only six weeks to enter the country or we would have to start the process over again. We still had to say good-byes to family in two states, pack up our household belongings into fifty-gallon drums, ship them to the far side of the world, and raise multiple thousands of dollars in financial support. It was the middle of November, which meant all this had to be done during the holidays.

It all seemed like very bad timing. Why had God delayed so long, and why had He chosen *now* to grant the visa? Once again we prayed over Psalm 50:15 and Philippians 4:19.

That week our church was sponsoring an annual missions conference, and as outgoing missionaries we got to eat dinner with the guest speaker. Over dinner we discussed our visa process and rejoiced with him about the visa being granted.

"So," he asked, "how is your financial support?"

I replied, "After three years of waiting, we now must enter within six weeks. I've got a ton of things to get done to move our family and say our good-byes, but the biggest hurdle seems to be our funding. We must be fully funded before we can leave. I need to raise $25,000 in the next six weeks." Just saying it out loud made it seem even more impossible.

During the message that evening this same speaker stopped his preaching and asked, "Where's that young couple with The Navigators who are going to Indonesia? Stand up!" We slowly rose to our feet in front of two thousand people, wondering what was about to happen. "Do you all see this couple?" he said, pointing us out to the crowd. "They've waited three years for a visa, and now it's been granted. But they still need $25,000 before they can leave. When I'm done speaking I want to see a line form in front of them with cash and checks in hand."

He told us to sit down. We sank into our seats not knowing what had just happened.

When the service ended, a mob formed around us. People stuffed cash and checks into our hands and pockets. They told us, "Whatever you need after you count it all, contact us."

That night we sat on our bed counting cash and checks. We had received almost $20,000! Within the week all of our financial needs were met! We packed and spent the holidays with both families before entering Indonesia, with a couple of days to spare.

An old story tells of a local minister who was visiting an older member of his congregation in her home. As they talked, the minister opened his Bible and began to share some passages of Scripture with the older woman. She followed in her Bible, which was well worn and contained much writing in the margins. The minister noted the used condition of her Bible and upon examining it found next to many passages the letters "T & P" written in the margins. Thinking this somewhat strange, he inquired as to the meaning.

"Oh, Pastor, those are my promises that I've marked," the old saint responded. "'T & P' simply means 'Tried and Proved.'"

The Lord invites us all to try and prove His promises, that

we might experience His faithfulness and love and that we might have testimonies to share with others about how we have come to know and serve a living God. Then we, too, will be able to testify with Spurgeon when he affirmed that he "believed all the promises of God but that many of them he had personally tried and proved."[3]

FOR THOUGHT AND DISCUSSION

Are you currently facing a trial of faith that is an opportunity to trust God and His promises? Practice praying over a promise that relates to your current situation. Come before your Father humbly and confidently. Pray Psalm 139:23-24 and confess any sins the Spirit helps you see. Lay out the details of your situation before God. Reflect to Him any of His promises or character traits that bear on your request. Consider before God any conditions required of you before He will fulfill His promises. Make your specific request. Repeat persistently.

5

WALKING BY FAITH WITH THE PROMISES

How many folks estimate difficulties in the light of their own resources, and thus attempt little and often fail in the little they attempt? All God's giants have been weak men and women, who did great things for God because they counted on His faithfulness.
HUDSON TAYLOR

How sweet are your words to my taste, sweeter than honey to my mouth!
PSALM 119:103

Your promises have been thoroughly tested, and your servant loves them.
PSALM 119:140

ONE OF OUR FAMILY TRADITIONS for Thanksgiving is the making of fresh butter. We purchase the cream, place it in a jar with a tight lid, and then shake it vigorously. The shaking usually wears out several people, as it seems that the cream will never turn. And then suddenly, in the instant of one shake, what was cream becomes a lump of delicious butter. Boy, does it taste good!

Making butter involves three essential elements: the cream, the jar, and the vigorous shaking over time. Similarly, seeing God answer our prayers over His promises involves three elements: the promises, faith, and patience. In Hebrews 6:12 we find these three elements applied to our prayers over the promises in His Word. "We do not want you to become lazy," the author writes, "but to imitate those who through faith and patience inherit what has been promised." Though it seems to take forever, the end result is worth the effort.

You can see these three elements in what I call the "Triangle for Triumph," for with these three components anyone will live a dynamic life in Christ.

Triangle for Triumph

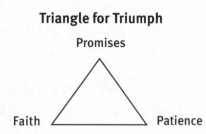

All three elements are necessary for a balanced, dynamic walk with God.

- Promises and faith without patience will lead to compromise and attempts to answer our own prayers.
- Promises and patience without faith will result in walking by sight, trusting in what is seen, and a lack of spiritual energy in our lives.

- Faith and patience without the promises of God is presumption and can lead to great hardship and error.

We must have all three—promises, faith, and patience—if we are to realize the blessings of God.

Faith

The promises alone, as great as they are, must be mixed with faith if we are to realize their fulfillment. The writer of Hebrews says,

> Therefore, since the promise of entering his rest still stands, let us be careful that none of you be found to have fallen short of it. For we also have had the gospel preached to us, just as they did; but the message they heard was of no value to them, because those who heard did not combine it with faith. (Hebrews 4:1-2)

Certainly the writer is referring to the promise of salvation, but the principle is true that *all* the promises of God must be combined with our faith in order to reach fulfillment.

Faith is not a feeling or an impression. It is not convincing ourselves of a truth, a kind of self-brainwashing. Faith is the simple acceptance and trust of what God has promised in the Scriptures. It is the acceptance and trust of a child; it is a trust that does not pay attention to the probabilities but sees only the promise and the Promiser and expectantly hopes. George Mueller distinguishes faith from more general impressions.

> Impressions come from human reasoning, which at best is untrustworthy. Faith, on the other hand, is based upon the impregnable Word of God. . . . The province of faith begins where probabilities cease and sight and sense fail.[1]

Biblical faith involves action: acting in accordance with what God has promised and acting to fulfill any conditions God has applied to the promise.

In 2 Corinthians 1:8-11, we can observe several principles related to walking by faith.

> We do not want you to be uninformed, brothers, about the hardships we suffered in the province of Asia. We were under great pressure, far beyond our ability to endure, so that we despaired even of life. Indeed, in our hearts we felt the sentence of death. But this happened that we might not rely on ourselves but on God, who raises the dead. He has delivered us from such a deadly peril, and he will deliver us. On him we have set our hope that he will continue to deliver us, as you help us by your prayers. Then many will give thanks on our behalf for the gracious favor granted us in answer to the prayers of many.

First of all, we note that Paul and his ministry team were not free from trials and testings. Those who seek to live godly lives in obedience to God's Word are not guaranteed a life free from cares and worries. Paul states that they were "under great pressure." The pressure was much more than they could bear, so much so that they even gave up hope of living through it. God not only allows times of trial and testing, but shows how they can be maximum faith-stretching experiences. He will bring us to points when we feel like giving up or caving in to compromise. These times are a normal part of God's training program for His children. Hebrews 12:11 says,

> No discipline seems pleasant at the time, but painful. Later on, however, it produces a harvest of righteousness and peace for those who have been trained by it.

Stated in today's vernacular, "No pain, no gain!"

Second, Paul unveils the reason for the great pressure they were experiencing; it was to teach them to "not rely on ourselves but on God." God was using this experience to build faith into Paul and his companions, teaching them to rely only on the all-powerful God who even raises the dead. If He can bring the dead to life, He can handle our present circumstances. As He declares to the prophet Jeremiah, "I am the LORD, the God of all mankind. Is anything too hard for me?" (Jeremiah 32:27).

Third, Paul testifies that God "has delivered us . . . will

deliver us," and "will continue to deliver us." That is, God has demonstrated His trustworthiness in the past, He will show it in our current situation, and we can also count on Him to be faithful in the future. The result is that many others would be encouraged and give praise to God for His answers to prayer, as they saw God's favor displayed toward Paul and his ministry team.

In high school I was active in many sports. As part of the off-season conditioning program for football we had to regularly lift weights. I can still remember the coach saying that it is not lifting the barbell one time with the most weight possible that builds strength. Rather, it is multiple repetitions with a lighter load, taking the muscles to the point of exhaustion, that builds muscle strength and endurance. Faith is similar in that the more often it is stretched and exercised the more it grows, enabling it to move a bigger load. We should not be discouraged if we often find ourselves in the midst of trying times, for it is through this repetition that the Lord builds the muscle of faith. God reminds us of His purposes in training us in faith when He says, "If you have raced with men on foot and they have worn you out, how can you compete with horses? If you stumble in safe country, how will you manage in the thickets by the Jordan?" (Jeremiah 12:5).

I'm reminded of yet another bit of wisdom from George Mueller:

Now, my beloved brothers and sisters, begin in a little way. At first, I was able to trust the Lord for ten dollars, then for a hundred dollars, then for a thousand dollars, then for one hundred thousand dollars, and now, with the greatest ease, I could trust Him for millions of dollars if there were occasion for it. But first, I should quietly, carefully, deliberately examine and see whether what I was trusting for, was something in accordance with His promises in His written Word. If I found it was, the amount of difficulties would be no hindrance to my trust.[2]

Patience

In addition to faith, we must add patience in order that we might receive what has been promised. We live in a day of instant gratification. Even instant is too slow for many of us! *Patience is for wimps. Go out and make something happen. Just do it!* Unfortunately, these principles are not in accordance with the plans of God.

Many times God seems to be slow in answering our prayers. We have the promises; we pray over the promises by faith and seek to meet any conditions stated. Yet God still does not answer. Why is He so slow? Is it that He is hard of hearing or asleep when we pray? Definitely not! Is it that we must convince God of our sincerity by praying for a long time? No, God sees our hearts and knows the end from the beginning, thus He knows my motives. Then why?

When God allows a delay, He's giving us more opportunities to trust, to walk by faith; we gain more time to exercise our muscle of faith. Once the answer comes, the opportunity to grow in faith is past. God is more interested in the process of our eternal sanctification than the resolution of one temporal situation.

One of my family's greatest faith-building experiences was during the three years that we waited for our Indonesian visa. While we waited, we moved to the southwest suburbs of Chicago to serve multiple churches in disciplemaking. This necessitated the prayerful hunt for another house rental with a month-to-month lease, as we did not know when the visa would come.

Once again our family of five made our prayer list— four bedrooms, near our home church, near the expressway around Chicago, easy access to the school, all appliances included, and a monthly rent for four hundred dollars.

One night as I prayed with Michael at bedtime, he said, "And remember, Jesus, I'm asking for a swimming pool and a swing set." I thought that this was a cute five-year-old's prayer and quickly concluded our prayer time. But Michael persisted in praying his two specific requests every night.

While visiting Chicago a few weeks before Michael's school would start, I was told of a pastor who had taken a church out of state and was trying to sell his house. I left information saying that if he would consider renting, I'd like to talk. I received a call the next day and soon had pulled up at an address five minutes from our church and the expressway. I could see that the home met many of the conditions on our prayer list.

After introductions I was shown around a beautiful four-bedroom home that had everything on our needs and desires list, including all appliances except a refrigerator. They agreed to a month-to-month rental arrangement and said that they only wanted to cover their mortgage payments of six hundred dollars. I acknowledged that this was a great deal, as market value was a minimum of two thousand per month.

Then I clarified that we could not afford six hundred. "So would you consider four hundred a month?" I asked. The pastor, his wife, and I knelt together and prayed for the Lord to show us what to do. I returned to Purdue and joined with Dana in praying specifically for this house.

A couple of days later our phone rang, and it was the house owner in Chicago. "I called you because we can't sleep."

"I don't understand," I said.

"Well, you're the reason. We think God wants us to rent this house to you, and it will cost us two hundred dollars for every month you live here. It just doesn't make good financial sense."

I agreed. But as we talked it became more and more evident that this was what God wanted for both of us. We agreed to rent the home, moving in the week before Michael was to start school. We rented there for three years while waiting for the visa, and the owners never raised the rent.

When I hung up the phone, my doorbell rang. I opened the door to see a pickup truck in my driveway with a new refrigerator in the back. Our friend at the door said, "We just bought a home that comes with all appliances. We've got this new refrigerator that we don't need and we'd like to give it to you. Do you want it?"

I smiled. "Ten minutes ago I would have said no, but actually I do need a refrigerator."

"Great," he said, "It's yours." And he unloaded it onto my porch.

We loaded our truck with our belongings and drove to our new rental in Chicago. I had Michael ride with me in the front of the truck. This was a big adventure for a little boy. When we pulled into the driveway of our new home, the families on both sides came out to greet us. Both of these homes had swimming pools in their backyards, and both neighbors told us that our children were welcome anytime.

"You see, Michael," I said to the wide-eyed boy. "You asked Jesus for a swimming pool, and He gave you two!" Then, hand in hand, we walked to the end of the drive and looked across the street at a complete playground full of swings, slides, jungle gyms, and roundabouts. "Michael, look," I whispered in his ear. "You asked Jesus for a swing set and He gave you a playground."

From then on I had a son who believed that Jesus can do anything!

We need to learn to enjoy each time of waiting, knowing that God is using it to build our confidence in Him and His promises. Our natural desire is to run from pressure and avoid the testing of our faith. It is painful living under the pressure of trials, but doing so brings beneficial results. Someone has said, "The mark of maturity is being able to enjoy the trip, even when you are on a detour." Job demonstrated wisdom when he, even in the midst of his horrible waiting, told his friends, "He knows the way that I take; when he has tested me, I will come forth as gold" (Job 23:10).

We must also recognize that our enemy, the Devil, is actively opposing us in our walk of faith. He is seeking to sow seeds of unbelief in the promises of God and to get us to doubt His reliability. One day Daniel began to pray and fast for understanding of a vision he had been given concerning the future of Israel (Daniel 10:1-14). For three weeks he waited until finally an angel arrived with the explanation. He had been sent with the answer from the first day Daniel began to pray, yet he was hindered in his arrival by "the prince of the Persian kingdom" (verse 13), generally understood to mean a fallen angel or territorial spirit. It was only after the arrival and assistance of the archangel Michael that the angel was able to break through to Daniel.

Now, Daniel did not know about the cosmic battle that was taking place as he prayed. He only knew that he had been praying and fasting for three weeks, and no answer had come. We, too, are often unaware of the cosmic forces that are warring as we pray. Trust that the Lord will answer in His perfect time; He has not forgotten!

Jesus taught in Matthew 7:7-8 that if we want to receive from God, we are to ask, seek, and knock. In the original language these verbs have the sense of continual action, not a onetime asking, seeking, or knocking. Jesus also told two parables, recorded in the gospel of Luke (11:5-8; 18:1-8), exhorting us to be persistent in prayer. We often give up too soon. God is omnipotent and omniscient; He knows no deadlines. His ability to see all things at once, compared to our limited ability, gives Him a much greater understanding as when best to act. Our man-made deadlines for God's answers may come and go, but when God finally does answer our prayers, we see that His timing is perfect. God is never late with His answers (2 Peter 3:9).

Why then does God ask us to pray persistently, setting before us those progressively intense tasks of asking, seeking, and knocking? Paul touches on this same truth in his first Thessalonian letter: "Be joyful always; pray continually" (1 Thessalonians 5:16-17). We pray continually and persistently, growing even more intense and bold in our requests, not to wear God down or to convince Him to give in to our desires, but because of the nature of prayer. As Bill Mills puts it,

> Praying without ceasing is walking in life with a sense
> of His presence. We are continually in fellowship
> with Him. As God draws us to Himself in prayer, we
> are encouraged, strengthened and transformed in the
> communion that we share with Him. In the intimacy
> that is ours as we pray together, our hearts become
> more and more like our Father's, and we begin to
> reflect His perspectives and responses.[3]

I am told that the Chinese language character for "perseverance" is actually a combination of two characters—one meaning "knife" and the other meaning "heart." Thus, for the Chinese, perseverance means "living with a knife in your heart." Often that is what it feels like as we wait upon God to answer. The pressure in that moment can seem unbearable. For times like those, Hebrews 10:36 bears repeating for the comfort it bestows: "You need to persevere so that when you have done the will of God, you will receive what he has promised."

Action

Whenever I speak on the subject of praying the promises, I invariably encounter questions like these: "But how do I know how much I'm supposed to work for the answer? Are you saying that all we need to do is pray, wait, and do nothing?"

No, I am not saying that. We are to pray as if it all depends upon God and work as if it all depends upon us.

I once counseled a man who was out of work. He needed a job to support his family, and we prayed together over Philippians 4:19, pleading it in prayer and asking the Lord to meet the man's need for a job. In addition to prayer, he made out a résumé and began to distribute it to various companies. It would have been wrong for him to simply pray and wait without making out the résumé and filling out the job applications. Both prayer and action were necessary, and the Lord provided him with a great job. When he got the new job, we did not praise the great résumé or the terrific way he had filled in the application forms. Rather we gave praise to God, who had answered yet another prayer.

A friend of mine has a painting of the Lord's disciples in a boat in the midst of rough waves on the Sea of Galilee. A storm is fast approaching, the waves are getting bigger, and the men have anxious looks on their faces. Under the painting is this caption: "Pray to God and row to shore." On the wall of my study I have a plaque that summarizes this principle in three little words: "Pray and Work." Both are part of walking by faith.

In order to obtain what God had promised, Noah had to build the ark and then enter it (Hebrews 11:7). Abraham had to leave his home and travel to a distant land (verse 8). The ten lepers Jesus healed had to go and show themselves to the priests (Luke 17:11-19). The disciples had to go back to Jerusalem and wait for ten days for the promised Holy Spirit before He was given on the Day of Pentecost (See Acts 1–2). All had to act upon their belief in the promise. Faith is active, not passive!

J. O. Fraser comments on the combination of faith and works:

> God gives us the ground in answer to the prayer of faith, but not the harvest. That must be worked for in cooperation with Him. Faith must be followed up by works. Prayer works. Salvation is of grace, but it must be worked out (Philippians 2:12) if it is to become ours. And the prayer of faith is just the same. It is given to us by free grace, but it will never be ours until we follow it up, work it out. Faith and

works must never be divorced, for indolence will reap no harvest in the spiritual world.[4]

And finally a word from A.W. Tozer concerning walking by faith:

> Though God dwells in the center of eternal mystery,
> there need be no uncertainty about how He will act in
> any situation covered by His promises. These promises
> are infallible predictions. God will always do what He
> has promised to do when His conditions are met. . . .
> A promise is only as good as the one who made it,
> but it is as good, and from this knowledge springs our
> assurance. By cultivating the knowledge of God we at
> the same time cultivate our faith.[5]

FOR THOUGHT AND DISCUSSION

Think of a promise you're praying over now (or one you've prayed in the past, but which hasn't yet been fulfilled). As you trust God and wait upon His answer, consider the following questions.

- Do you believe God can and will fulfill His promise?
- Are you willing to persist patiently in praying this promise—maybe your whole life?
- Are you willing to take any next steps of faith as part of God's answer?

Based on your answers to these three questions, what can you do (in dependence on God) to continue to walk by faith in this journey?

6

ABUSES AND UNFULFILLED PROMISES

Prayer is not overcoming God's reluctance; it is laying hold of His highest willingness.
RICHARD C. TRENCH

But how to get faith strengthened? Not by striving after faith, but by resting on the Faithful One.
HUDSON TAYLOR

THE SUBJECT OF PRAYING PROMISES often meets with a negative reaction, or at least a reluctant hesitancy. I hear all kinds of objections:

- "Is it right to pray for ourselves a promise that was given at another time to someone else?"
- "This sounds suspiciously like putting God to the test."
- "I've had bad experiences with people taking a verse out of context and calling it God's voice."

How can we answer these objections and maintain our spiritual balance when praying God's promises?

Abuses

So many of God's good gifts can be abused. Unfortunately, His promises are among these. We'll examine only a few of the more common ways of misusing the promises of Scripture.

Prosperity Theology

A common movement today in many Christian circles is known as "prosperity theology." Those who hold this conviction believe that it is God's will for all believers to be materially prosperous. Ken Sarles defines it as follows:

> Prosperity theology is not a denomination, a
> tradition, or even a school of thought. It is a broadly
> based, variegated movement that overlaps both the
> charismatic and non-charismatic spectrums. . . .
> Perhaps the major emphases of this movement can
> best be summarized by rewording the old adage
> about being healthy, wealthy, and wise. In this case
> the good news of the prosperity gospel is how to be
> healthy, wealthy, and demon-free.[1]

With their misplaced confidence in their chosen outcome, those who subscribe to prosperity theology make dramatic overtures of faith: They stop taking medication for illnesses, for example, or refuse treatment for cancer. "God will heal me," they tell their friends, "because I have faith." This is not faith, but foolishness! It is presumption, not praying the promises.

When we talk about pleading promises in prayer we are *not* talking about a "name it and claim it" belief system. God does not promise us a carefree or trouble-free life, even if we walk in obedience to Him and seek to live in dependence on Him. There is no promise of prosperity for all believers. The clearest example to the contrary is that of Jesus Himself. Jesus led a morally perfect life: sinless, in complete submission and obedience to the Father. Yet He died an early death by crucifixion, and at His death His only possession was His robe. This was hardly a prosperous life by the world's terms.

Promise claiming does not give us the right to expect that we will always experience the world's best, but it does give us the right to expect *God's* best. Consider John 16:24: "Until now you have not asked for anything in my name. Ask and you will receive, and your joy will be complete."

Some people take this to mean that if I have faith enough to ask, then I can be assured that God will do what I ask. By extension, if God does not do as I ask, then it is my fault for lacking enough faith. While God does promise to answer all of our prayers, He does *not* promise to always say yes to our requests when He has not promised the outcome. Even His own Son was told no three times when He asked for deliverance from the cross (Matthew 26:36-44), because the Father had never promised such deliverance. Paul, who healed many and even raised Eutychus back to life (Acts 20:9-12), left Trophimus sick on Miletus (2 Timothy 4:20). Paul asked God to heal him of his "thorn in my flesh" three times, but was told no, because no such healing was promised; Paul eventually realized the hidden blessing in this affliction (2 Corinthians 12:6-10). Like Jesus and Paul, we can boldly ask for everything (Philippians 4:6-7), but we do so with a humble submission to God's will for us, trusting in His love, goodness, and sovereignty.

God can and does heal people miraculously, and I have been a part of some amazing healing stories. But I have also been part of life stories in which people have been prayed for and anointed with oil (see James 5:14), and they have still died from their illnesses. Going to a physician for an illness is not sin or a lack of faith. Whether God heals miraculously or through the hand of a physician, both are His answer to our prayer of faith. All healing finds its source in Him, and we praise Him no matter what means He uses. We also praise Him by faith, in an attitude of submission and trust, if He says no to our request for healing, trusting that He knows best and that all He does is good. Nothing touches me outside of His good and perfect will for me. I can find peace and rest in this truth. *That's* biblical faith.

Putting God to the Test

Another legitimate concern when pleading promises is the fear of putting God to the test. We remember Jesus' rebuke of Satan when the deceiver tempted Him to throw Himself off the highest point of the temple (Matthew 4:5-7). The Devil quoted a promise (Psalm 91:11-12), implying that no harm would come to Jesus because of God's promised care. Jesus rebuked Satan by quoting Deuteronomy 6:16, saying, "Do not put the Lord your God to the test" (Matthew 4:7).

Certainly living by faith is an expected lifestyle for all followers of Christ. In Habbakuk 2:4 we read, "The righteous will live by his faith." This passage is repeated three times in the New Testament. When God repeats Himself, we need to pay very close attention. Thus, when we find ourselves in frequent trials of faith where we are thrust into dependence on Him for provision or protection, we should not be surprised. The storms of life come to those who build their house on the sand as well as those who build on the rock (Matthew 7:24-27).

But this does not mean that we should put God to the test, demanding that He do things for us because we are taking steps of faith. James reminds us that "God cannot be tempted by evil, nor does he tempt anyone" (James 1:13). We are clay, and God is the potter (Isaiah 64:8); He has the right to do as He sees fit (Psalm 115:3).

It would seem that our attitude is a key factor in determining whether we are praying in faith or demanding something from God and violating the command not to put God to the test. In some passages the Lord encourages us to take Him up on His promises, to test them and see if they are true:

Bring the whole tithe into the storehouse, that there may be food in my house. Test me in this . . . and see if I will not throw open the floodgates of heaven and pour out so much blessing that you will not have room enough for it. (Malachi 3:10)

When pleading promises in prayer, we are not seeking to bind God in some solemn oath, forcing Him to act according to our own desires, as the Devil was seeking to do when tempting Jesus. Rather, we come to God in humility and reverence, acknowledging His lordship over us and His right to act as He pleases. We come pleading with Him to fulfill His promises, not demanding that He perform according to our wishes. God will not jump through our hoops like some trained circus animal, no matter how advantageous we may think the answers are for the advance of the kingdom. We cannot purposely place ourselves in desperate situations and expect the Lord to deliver us. He will not be forced by us into acting a certain way. Yet if we do find ourselves in desperate circumstances, we can confidently plead the promises of God for peace, strength, protection, and the like, knowing that He will watch over us and care for us.

Fleshly Desires

Another fear of abuse when pleading promises relates to Psalm 106:14-15:

In the desert they [Israel] gave in to their craving;
    in the wasteland they put God to the test.
So he gave them what they asked for,
    but sent a wasting disease upon them.

The concern is that perhaps our pleading of the promises is motivated by desires arising from our flesh. Perhaps as I diligently pray over these promises, God will answer yes, even though He knows that what I desire will fail to benefit me, and may even harm me. Or perhaps the Lord will give me the beneficial desires of my flesh, but also discipline me for my wrong motives.

At first glance that is what seemed to happen to the Israelites. It would appear that they wearied God by their constant complaining about a lack of meat, and God finally relented and sent an abundance of quail. But along with the quail, He also sent a disease that killed many of them. This interpretation sees this episode as a kind of object lesson: "Don't ask for your desires, for you may get more than you ask for!" But is this what really happened?

In Psalm 78:17-31 we find another recounting of the same incident: "They willfully put God to the test by demanding the food they craved" (verse 18); the Israelites challenged God's ability to provide for them in the midst of the desert. "They did not believe in God or trust in his deliverance" (verse 22). In response to their sinful attitudes,

> He rained meat down on them like dust,
> flying birds like sand on the seashore.
> He made them come down inside their camp,
> all around their tents.
> They ate till they had more than enough,
> for he had given them what they craved.

But before they turned from the food they craved,
> even while it was still in their mouths,
> God's anger rose against them;
he put to death the sturdiest among them,
> cutting down the young men of Israel. (verses 27-31)

Thus, we see that it was their sinful, demanding attitudes that brought the wrath of God on them, not the request itself.

Contrary to the "Don't pray for your desires" school of thought, Jesus encouraged us to make bold requests.

> Which of you, if his son asks for bread, will give
> him a stone? Or if he asks for a fish, will give him a
> snake? If you, then, though you are evil, know how
> to give good gifts to your children, how much more
> will your Father in heaven give good gifts to those
> who ask him! (Matthew 7:9-11)

In other words, because our Father loves us and wants what is best for us, He will not respond to any of His children's requests with something that would be detrimental for us. He loves us too much for that.

Suppose one of my three children came to me and said, "Dad, I'd like you to give me a hand grenade for my birthday." How would I respond? Obviously, because of the danger, I would not grant the request, even if my beloved child continued to plead, saying, "But I really, really want a hand grenade, Dad! Please get me one!" Though he or she would ask me a thousand times (even with fasting), I would not say yes to that desire. Why? Not because I'm not capable or because I don't want to meet my children's requests. The reason I don't give them something harmful, even when they ask for it, is because I love them too much. According to Jesus, if we who are evil and fallen in our natures can show that kind of reasoning and love, how much more will the love of our heavenly Father prevent Him from answering a request with something that will bring us harm.

James 4:3 says, "When you ask, you do not receive, because you ask with wrong motives, that you may spend what you get on your pleasures." If we are seeking something with wrong motives, James says, we won't get it. That is all; God will say, "Sorry, but the answer to that request is no." He will not add, "And I will teach you never to ask for something like that again, you terrible person!" We simply won't get what we request.

Proof Texting

Another abuse often seen in connection with praying promises is taking a passage out of context and seeking to use it as a proof text for some desired outcome of our own devising. Given our human creativity, we are capable of freely associating any and every meaning from any passage. I have sought to balance this error by repeating the need to use good hermeneutics—the historical-grammatical approach—when pleading a promise. We must know the meaning of any passage to the original audience before we can begin to seek application for our own lives. We must know the Scriptures in their entirety so that we will not be led off into some false teaching or some extreme that would take us out of God's will. The whole interprets the part, and any part must be interpreted with respect to the whole of Scripture. This calls for maturity in Christ and a submission to His lordship when pleading promises.

Augustine was a great man of God, very mature in the Lord and very knowledgeable in the Scriptures. His allegorical approach to interpretation led him to many insights from God's Word. Unfortunately, his disciples who came after him were not as well grounded in the Bible and tended to run to excess using the same allegorical methods. Though we ourselves may understand the principles of praying promises, we must insure that those who would copy our example are well-grounded and balanced in their use of the Word.

Warren Myers provides four reminders of some "dangers in going to Scripture looking for some verse to 'leap out,' as conclusive guidance in finding God's will (or confirming it, or solving a current problem)":[2]

1. Finding such passages can become our main motive in going to the Bible. This can keep us from learning truths God wants us to know and can hinder our applying "less spectacular" verses.

2. We can substitute this "easy" method of finding guidance for mature, careful determining of God's will in making decisions.

3. It is easy to find confirmation of what we want. It is possible to prove almost anything through wrongly used Scripture. The promises of God are not a means to force God into doing what we want done, but the means by which God reveals what He wants and expects. They are for the purpose of fulfilling God's will, not ours.

4. Unwise praying of promises can lead to disappointment, confusion, and even doubt of the Bible's trustworthiness. If a personal promise isn't fulfilled, we may doubt God's faithfulness or we may be discouraged by our immaturity in discerning God's will and appropriating His promises.

Unfulfilled Promises

We must accept the fact that not all promises that we plead in prayer will be answered. Why? The following are a few reasons for unfulfilled promises.

Disobedience

Disobedience is perhaps the most common reason for unfulfilled promises. We must be living obedient lives under the lordship of Christ if we are to see many of His promises realized. John MacArthur comments:

Israel was able to have complete hope in God's promises because He had every resource at His disposal and because He cannot lie. They had God's promises, and they knew He was able and trustworthy to fulfill them. The fact that they often failed to hope in those promises was due to their own unfaithfulness, not God's.[3]

Many promises are conditional, demanding that we meet certain requirements before we receive the promised blessing. Adam was promised the opportunity to live forever in the Garden of Eden and to enjoy fellowship with God, but there was a condition. He was never to eat from the Tree of Knowledge of Good and Evil. If he disobeyed, then the promise would not be fulfilled. Of course we know what happened, and Adam, through his disobedience, lost the promise of avoiding death.

Similarly, Luke 6:38 says, "Give, and it will be given to you. . . . For with the measure you use, it will be measured to you." In this conditional promise we have to first give to God before we can expect anything to be given to us. If we are disobedient in our giving, God is under no obligation to fulfill His part of the promise. We must remain under the lordship of Christ, seeking Him first in all areas and yielded to His will for our lives. We must remain filled with the Spirit, under His control. MacArthur again states,

The work of the Holy Spirit in us and on our behalf can be appropriated only as He fills us. Every Christian is indwelt by the Holy Spirit and has the potential of receiving the fulfillment of all Christ's promises to those who belong to Him. But no Christian will have those promises fulfilled who is not under the full control of the Holy Spirit.[4]

Unbelief

Unbelief is the opposite of faith; it refuses to accept or act upon obvious truth that is presented. Unbelief will stop us from asking or pleading the promises in prayer.

In Mark 6:1-6, Jesus returned to his hometown of Nazareth. On the Sabbath He went to the synagogue and began to preach, and many were impressed with his knowledge of the Scriptures and His teachings (verses 1-2). Yet they began to question where this wisdom could have come from (verses 2-3). They knew Him as a carpenter's son, a boy they had seen numerous times playing with His brothers as He grew up in the village. Yes, He had wisdom, but where could He have gotten it? They refused to accept the obvious. The result was that Jesus "could not do any miracles there, except lay his hands on a few sick people and heal them. And he was amazed at their lack of faith" (verses 5-6). Their unbelief or lack of faith thus limited their willingness to ask Him for help and limited Jesus' ability to bless them.

Our unbelief in the promises of God will also cause us not to plead them by faith in prayer and thus will limit what God could do in and through us. James reminds us, "You do not have, because you do not ask God" (James 4:2).

Lack of Patience

Another common reason for unfulfilled promises is our lack of perseverance or patience. As I mentioned in chapter 5, three components are necessary for us to see God's answers: promises, faith, and patience. When the answer seems long in coming, we are often lured into compromise, or we seek to answer the prayer by our own means. J. O. Fraser comments,

> Is not this another secret of many unanswered prayers—that they are not fought through? If the result is not seen as soon as expected, Christians are apt to lose heart and, if it is still longer delayed, to abandon it altogether. We must count the cost before praying the prayer of faith. We must be willing to pay the price. We must mean business. We must set ourselves to "see things through" (Ephesians 6:18, "with all perseverance").[5]

In chapter 2 I shared an answer to prayer for a bookcase, but there is more to the story. The day of the provision we were driving in the country and passed a pile of used bricks on the side of the road. I stopped the car and examined the bricks. They were plain, dirty, red bricks, covered with cement, yet I thought that this was God's answer. Sure it wasn't exactly what I was trusting Him for. *But hey, let's not get too choosy*, I thought. *Besides, we really need those shelves, and I can always find some boards somewhere.* So I loaded my trunk and came home planning to spend the next day cleaning the bricks. You can imagine my shock when later that night my neighbor offered us his bookcase. When I compared my own answer with what the Lord had obviously provided, I was deeply embarrassed and humbled.

The Lord taught me a valuable lesson that day—one that I have seen repeated often as we walk by faith. When the answer is near, the opportunities for compromise increase. The Enemy will bring many things into our lives that are close to what we are trusting God for, but not exactly it. When you find this happening, be encouraged, for the answer will be arriving soon. Don't give in to compromise! Strengthen your faith and keep trusting. Jesus told His disciples the parable of the persistent widow, Luke tells us, "to show them that they should always pray and not give up" (Luke 18:1). It's always too soon to give up on God's promises.

Misclaiming the Promise

We must acknowledge that sometimes we do simply misclaim the promises. Perhaps we do not interpret the Scriptures correctly, or we do not discern God's will for us accurately. We must review the integrity of our motives.

Seeking mature counsel is a good safeguard. Let us heed this reminder from Warren Myers:

> If you share your special promises with others,
> acknowledge that this is your personal application,
> not the actual meaning of the verse. Avoid being

dogmatic. Acknowledge clearly the subjective element in praying the promise for specific things. Later on, if necessary, be ready to admit that you were mistaken in the way you applied the passage. Even Paul made occasional mistakes in discerning God's will—Acts 16:7; 2 Corinthians 12:8-9.

It might be wise to encourage new believers to stay with God's general promises for a while— especially those in the New Testament.[6]

It has been my experience that as I pray over certain promises, if I am in the will of God, there will be within my heart a confirmation: *This is right. Press on.* The opposite has also been true: When I am out of the will of God while pleading a certain promise, or if the answer is no, I will sense a lack of peace, and the desire to believe the promise will wane. If we are yielded to God, seeking His glory and His best and not our own, He is very capable of leading us and keeping us in the center of His will for our lives. His reputation is at stake, and He will guide us so that we may bring glory to His name.

FOR THOUGHT AND DISCUSSION

As you reflect upon this chapter, choose one of the abuses, attitudes, or bad habits that you know you're prone to fall into. Take some time to talk honestly about it with your Father. What practical steps can you take—in prayer and in other aspects of your life—to address it?

7

ABRAHAM: ONE WHO
TRUSTED THE PROMISES

*It doesn't matter, really, how great the pressure is, it only matters where
the pressure lies. See that it never comes between you and the Lord—
then, the greater the pressure, the more it presses you to His breast.*

HUDSON TAYLOR

*Yet [Abraham] did not waver through unbelief regarding the promise
of God, but was strengthened in his faith and gave glory to God, being
fully persuaded that God had power to do what he had promised.*

ROMANS 4:20-21

I GAZED ANGRILY, forlornly out the airplane window.
Indonesia—our family's home and ministry location for the
last eleven years—was disappearing below us. Dear friends
and kingdom opportunities, all yanked away in a matter of
weeks. Why? Because I refused to pay a bribe to the official who could have granted us Indonesian citizenship and
another ten years in the country.

Why, God? I prayed. *Didn't You call us here? We worked so hard to get here and stay here, year after year. You answered so many prayers to make this happen. I feel like we were just getting started. Where are You in all this? Don't you want experienced, fruitful missionaries who love to be here?*

Indonesia had been our "Promised Land." I wonder if this was how Abram felt. God had promised him a fruitful land and even led him and his family there. Then came a famine in that blessed land (Genesis 12:10), and they were forced to leave and find refuge in Egypt. Abraham left on camelback, not on an airplane. But I think I can identify with the disillusionment he likely felt upon his departure, only a few years after arriving in this promised place. *Where is God's provision? Why would God lead us to a place and then force us to leave? Isn't this where He led us and promised to bless us?* There were no clear answers, for Abram or for me—only the reality that God was leading and that His promised blessing still remained backed by His power and character.

What stung the most for my family was the dashing of the high expectations we had had only a couple of months earlier. After more than a decade of residency, we were comfortable with the language and the culture, and our ministry was touching many lives. We now met the qualifications for Indonesian citizenship; we could hold dual passports for the next ten years. No more yearly renewals—now we finally could make some long-term plans.

Then came the immigration official who demanded a large bribe to process our paperwork. Because I refused to pay, we got a letter from his office stating that our application for citizenship had been denied and that we had six weeks to leave the country.

As we had done so often before, we prayed over Psalm 50:15, recruited prayer, and expectantly waited for the Lord to once again deliver us at the last hour. I was certain that, just as we had seen Him do many times before, this time once again He would somehow, someway deliver us in this time of trouble. But six weeks later we sat on a plane headed back to the United States.

Needless to say, it was a long, long airplane ride back home. I was angry, but I did not know who to be angry with. Corrupt officials? The Devil? Yes, I even considered God as a target for my frustration. Maybe I could have bargained with that official (we bargained for everything in Indonesia) and paid a much lower price? But would I really want to be someplace serving God, knowing that I had to bribe an official to stay there?

Someone once said, "God's will is what you would choose if you knew everything that He knows." But we don't. That's why we cling to the Word that He chooses to reveal—especially His promises.

Uprooted in Faith

Like me, I'm sure Abram had a lot of questions in his life. Especially at the "beginning," when he was about seventy years old. Abram lived in Mesopotamia (modern-day Iraq) in the city of Ur, an urban center known for its wealth and culture. It was here that God spoke to him for the first time: "Leave your country and your people . . . and go to the land I will show you" (Acts 7:3). Abram, his wife Sarai, his father, and his nephew Lot responded by moving from Ur to the city of Haran, seven hundred miles to the northwest, located today in Turkey near the Syrian border.

Haran was a flourishing city, located on one of the major caravan trade routes. Abram lived here until the death of his father. Then God spoke to Abram a second time, again telling him to leave his country, friends, relatives, and immediate family and to go to a place that God would later show him (Genesis 12:1-3). In addition to the command to leave, God promised to make him a great nation, to make his name great, to bless him and make him a blessing, to protect him. Further, God promised that through Abram *all* peoples of earth would be blessed.[1] Abram was seventy-five years old at this time (verse 4). He responded to God's promise by leaving Haran with his remaining family, along with his possessions (verse 5).

It was God who took the initiative with Abram. It was God who sought Abram out and of His own accord made the personal promise to him and his offspring. We do not go looking for personal promises; they will come as we walk with God and as He sovereignly chooses to bestow them. We do not play "Bible roulette"—standing the Bible on its spine and letting it fall open to a page and expecting God to give us a promise. Nor do we open the Word demanding God give us a promise as a sign of His leading. We walk by faith, not by sight! We come to the Bible with an expectant attitude that its Author will speak to us as we regularly interact with God through His Word.

We also note that though the promise had great potential, it still required obedience on Abram's part to appropriate it. He would not have realized that great potential if he stayed in Haran. The Scriptures say that, "By faith Abraham . . . obeyed and went, even though he did not know where he was going" (Hebrews 11:8). Unless we obey the leading the Lord gives us today, we may not have opportunity to be led tomorrow. We may not have enough light to see to the end of the road, but we do have enough light for the next step, and God expects us to take it. He will give us additional light when needed as we continue to move ahead. Unfortunately, many believers are paralyzed by fear of the future, wanting to know how everything will work out. The result is that they never take that first step of faith.

Pursuing a Promise

Abram traveled southwest and eventually arrived in Shechem in Palestine, a trip of approximately 450 miles. Here God spoke to him for the third time, assuring Abram that this land would be given to his offspring (Genesis 12:7). Abram responded by building an altar and worshiping God near the town of Bethel.

It was at this time that the family traveled to Egypt due to the famine in Palestine, but this was only a temporary setback: Abram returned with greatly increased wealth. God spoke to Abram for the fourth time at the same site as that of the third visitation. He once again reassured Abram that the land would be given to him and his offspring forever, that his offspring would be numerous, and that he should not be afraid to explore the land (Genesis 13:14-17). Abram responded by moving to Hebron and again building an altar to the Lord.

Observe the number of times the Lord sought to reassure Abram about the reality of the fulfillment of the promise. Our Lord knows that when the answer is long in coming, we tend to doubt and want to give up hope. We can expect that as we walk by faith with the promises, the Lord will reconfirm these promises in our hearts, even though there may be no visible reason to believe that they are being fulfilled. The eyes of faith will focus on the promise and the Promiser, not on the circumstances, as we wait for the answer. "So we fix our eyes not on what is seen, but on what is unseen" (2 Corinthians 4:18). The Scriptures say concerning Abraham that "by faith . . . he considered him faithful who had made the promise" (Hebrews 11:11). George Mueller reminds us that one of the conditions of answered prayer is "faith in God's word of promise as confirmed by His oath. Not to believe Him is to make Him both a liar and a perjurer."[2]

Abram returned to Hebron, and God spoke to him a fifth time in a vision (Genesis 15:1-21). God encouraged him not to be afraid and promised a son who would be his heir and that his descendants would be as many as the stars in the sky (verses 4-5). The Lord reminded Abram that He had brought him out of Ur for the purpose of giving him the land. He again promised Abram and his descendants the land, but only after a wait of four hundred years (verses 13, 16). Abram initially questioned God as to the promise's fulfillment, knowing that he was growing old and still had no child. Yet, "Abram believed the Lord, and he credited it to him as righteousness" (verse 6). Abram asked God for some assurance that these things would come to pass, and the Lord then made a covenant with him to this end (verse 18).

Fear about the future seems to have been one of Abraham's character flaws, and the Lord sought to reassure him, telling him not to be afraid. If we find ourselves fearful about the future or wondering about how the Lord can possibly bring to pass what He has promised, this is normal. If we could figure out how the answer would come, there would be no need for faith. Fear is not sin! Unbelief, not doubt, is sin. Doubt only needs more information and encouragement to believe, and we can expect God to meet these needs as we walk by faith. We can expect God to clarify His promises to us as we walk in them.

God will stretch us in our faith, but He will not break us!

As a father has compassion on his children,
    so the Lord has compassion on those who fear him;
for he knows how we are formed,
    he remembers that we are dust. (Psalm 103:13-14)

> He tends his flock like a shepherd:
>> He gathers the lambs in his arms
>> and carries them close to his heart;
> he gently leads those that have young. (Isaiah 40:11)

I often remind the Lord of my own impatience, my desire to give up or to doubt His promises as I walk with Him. During those times I ask Him to help me believe and not give up hoping. And as I see my ability to wait ebbing away or my capacity to stand the pressure beginning to wilt, I remind the Lord of His promise: "A bruised reed he will not break, and a smoldering wick he will not snuff out" (Isaiah 42:3). Be real with Him when you pray, and do not try to put up a brave front. That's not real faith. God knows our hearts. Share your feelings when you pray. Abraham had his doubts, and so will we.

Privileged to Be Patient

In Genesis 16, Abram was now eighty-five years old (verse 3), and had walked by faith with the promises of God for ten years. He had left all, and God had brought him to a new land, but he still had no heir according to the promise of God. During the past ten years God had spoken with him on five occasions, encouraging him and strengthening him to continue and reaffirming His promises. Abram seems to have run out of perseverance, however, and settled for a compromise, trusting in his own ability to discern God's answer. He had a son, Ishmael, through his wife's maidservant, Hagar, thinking that this would surely be the Lord's answer.

Just like Abraham, we get impatient when the Lord takes a long time to answer. Because He is outside of time, to the Lord "a day is like a thousand years, and a thousand years are like a day" (2 Peter 3:8). God knows no deadlines, for He is omnipotent. He can do whatever is necessary to meet or change any deadline as He pleases. And the Lord will often take longer to answer than we think is necessary. But remember that He is using the process of waiting to build Christlike character into our lives. This process is more important than the answer.

We learned this the third time we applied for our yearly visa renewal in Indonesia. We had lived there for two years, and it was again time to apply for official permission to stay another year. Because of national elections and holidays our paperwork was late in being processed. Our temporary visa extension expired, and when I went to the city immigration office to ask for another temporary extension, I was told that we could not obtain one. We were politely asked to leave the country! I immediately appealed the decision and asked for a letter of introduction to the regional immigration office to plead my case.

The letter of introduction from city immigration stated that we had overstayed our visa and that they objected to our being given any consideration for further extension. We prayed over Psalm 50:15 and recruited prayer. Then, along with another Indonesian staff, I carried the offending letter to the regional immigration office to face an official who had a reputation of being very hard on missionaries.

As we pulled the car into the parking lot, the personnel in the office began to file out. It immediately became obvious that this was not a greeting for us, but rather for the man in the car that pulled in behind ours. We checked and found that this was the first day of work for a new regional immigration office head, and his staff were out to welcome him to the office. We inquired about the possibility of seeing him, but were given little hope, as he was in meetings all day.

We decided to sit on a bench in a hallway that would give us a view of several offices, hoping to catch the official between meetings. Several hours passed with no sign of the office head. Then a door opened and out he came. We jumped up and rushed toward him, hoping to gain his attention before he disappeared once again behind another door. He greeted us and ushered us into his office. We were his first official business in his new capacity.

We explained our situation, and, after he learned that I was a missionary, he acknowledged that he too was a believer. He was most understanding of our situation and granted us another two-month temporary extension. Our papers were finally finished several weeks afterward and the new yearly visa granted.

I often reflect on God's timing when I think about this experience. Why did God make us wait, delaying the temporary extension? Certainly He had the power to grant our extension at any time. But when we were faced with expulsion from the country, He brought in a new regional office head whose heart He had prepared to help us. Had I gone to the office even one day earlier, I would have had to face the other official, who no doubt would not have been as helpful. God does know what He is doing, even though at times we wonder!

On the Eve of Fulfillment

In Genesis 17 Abram was now ninety-nine years old and still living in Hebron, having walked with God for twenty-four years since the original promise in Haran. God spoke to him for the sixth time and assured him that the promise would be fulfilled. Abram's name was changed to Abraham ("father of a multitude") and Sarai to Sarah. The Lord clarified further the promise of the land and that within a year Sarah would give birth to a son who would be named Isaac (verse 21). Abraham responded by falling face down in worship two times (verses 3,17), yet he still wondered how the Lord would fulfill the promise, seeing that he and Sarah were now well advanced in age (verse 17). But he obeyed the Lord by circumcising himself and every male in his household, as was the condition of the promise (verses 23-27).

Many of God's promises may seem illogical or impossible. It is not for us to decide the details or a probability of God's working. It is enough for us to believe. He will answer in such a way that He alone will receive the glory; for all who see it will have to acknowledge that only God could do such a thing. J. O Sanders reminds us,

> The prayer of faith has its basis in neither outward circumstances nor inward feelings. It is when sight brings no helpful vision and comfortable emotions are largely absent that the prayer of faith finds its greatest opportunity. It springs from the naked promise or affirmation of the Word of God, for faith proceeds only from a divine warrant. The prayer of faith is the power which converts promise into performance.[3]

By Genesis 18, Abraham was visited for the seventh time by the Lord and two angels, who were on their way to destroy Sodom and Gomorrah. The Lord promised to return within the year, and in that span of time a son would be born to Sarah (verse 10). Sarah doubted the promise due to her extreme age, but God repeated it, softly rebuking her, testifying to His ability to do anything He promises and affirming that surely she would have a son within the year (verses 13-14). Abraham fellowshiped with the Lord, and this time he showed no sign of questioning the promise.

"Now the LORD was gracious to Sarah as he had said, and the LORD did for Sarah what he had promised" (Genesis 21:1). Isaac, the son of the promise, was born when Abraham was one hundred years old, twenty-five years after the original promise was given (verse 5). Between the time of the giving of the original promise in Haran until the birth of Isaac, God had spoken to Abraham seven times, reassuring him that all would come to pass as promised.

Abraham finally died at the age of 175 (Genesis 25:7). Having lived for one hundred years from the time of the original promise in Haran, he had seen the marriage of Isaac to Rebekah and the birth of his grandchildren Jacob and Esau (when he was 160 years young, verse 26). Thus Abraham was able to see his two grandchildren grow to be young men before he died. But Abraham died having seen only two generations—a total of three people (Isaac, Jacob, and Esau)—though the Lord had promised offspring as numerous as the stars in the sky. God spoke to Abraham a total of nine times during his last hundred years (the seven mentioned previously, plus God's command to sacrifice Isaac and His command to stop), but during approximately the last sixty years of his life—since the testing of the sacrifice of Isaac—we have no record of God speaking with Abraham.

Special life promises may be few and far between. Don't get discouraged if God's special promises to you are few in number. Also note that the final fulfillment of some promises may be left for succeeding generations. Abraham did not see the total fulfillment of his promised many offspring, except that he saw them with the eyes of faith.

The following is a chronology of God's promise to multiply Abraham, and the promise's fulfillment. Yes, the Lord was faithful to fulfill the promise, but note the lengths of time involved!

God's Promise of a People to Abram

Genesis 12:1	God's command to Abram to leave Ur
Genesis 12:2-3	God's promise to Abram in Haran
Genesis 12:7	God's promise renewed at Shechem
Genesis 13:14-18	God's promise renewed again
Genesis 15:1	Ten years later; encouragement
Genesis 16	Abram impatient after waiting eleven years for the answer; Ishmael is born
Genesis 17	Reassurance and name changed to Abraham
Genesis 18:15	Promise of a son within the year
Genesis 21:5	Twenty-five years after the promise, Isaac is born; *now there are three people.*
Genesis 23:1	Sarah dies; *now there are two.*
Genesis 24	Isaac marries; *now there are three.*
Genesis 25:7-8	Abraham dies one hundred years later; *now there are four.* (Jacob and Esau were born when Abraham was 160 years old.)
Genesis 26:3-4	Renewal of promise to Isaac
Genesis 29-30, 35	*Jacob has twelve sons and their families,* 191 years after the promise was given.
Exodus 12:37,41	*After Egypt, there were two-plus million people,* 621 years after the promise was given (430 years + 191 years = 621 years).
Galatians 3:6-9	*Now, four millennia since Abraham, his "children" are as numerous as the stars in the sky and the sand on the seashore.*

Divine Detour

We are now twenty years from our devastating plane ride home to America, and it's very clear in retrospect what the Lord was doing when we were forced out of Indonesia. We landed back in America and were asked to join The Navigators' collegiate ministry leadership team. Within a couple of years we were leading the national collegiate work. This led to another decade of coaching student ministry leaders internationally and now a role on the US national leadership team for The Navigators, where we lead our Nations initiatives.

The Lord used that visa "disaster" to redirect us into something that hadn't even been a consideration for us. Now I'm grateful for that trial of faith, and this reflection serves today as a reminder to continue to trust Him—especially when life doesn't seem to make sense from my limited perspective. The Lord is sovereign, He is good, and He can be trusted.

By faith and perseverance we will see the promises of God fulfilled. Don't give up! Take to heart the words of Jesus: "Don't be afraid; just believe" (Mark 5:36).

FOR THOUGHT AND DISCUSSION

God knows the perfect way and the perfect time to answer when you pray one of His promises. Often His timetable is longer than we desire, and His method of answering might be different from what we expect. Talk with Him about your willingness to accept His timing and manner of answering. Voice your frustration if necessary; He can handle it. Now recommit to continue praying and living in confident, submissive expectancy.

Conclusion

GOD WANTS DEPENDENT CHILDREN, not independent ones! He desires that we depend on Him daily. And as a source of encouragement to do so, He has given us many, many promises. These promises are given that He may demonstrate His goodness and faithfulness and to glorify Himself through their fulfillment. J. I. Packer writes,

> As Father, Husband and King (these are the human
> models in terms of which His covenant relationship
> is presented), God is faithful to His promise and
> purpose, and the promise itself—the promise to be
> "your God," "a God unto thee"—is a comprehensive
> promise which, when unpacked, proves to contain

within itself all the "exceeding great and precious promises" in which God has pledged Himself to meet our needs.[1]

God wants to be everything for the believer; He can and will meet all of our needs—physical, spiritual, and emotional—if we trust Him.

The Lord is waiting for us to take Him up on His "great and precious promises" (2 Peter 1:4). Like precious gems they await our discovery and possession. But just as gemstones must be cut and polished, so we must add to these promises faith and patience if we are to see the brilliance of their fulfillment. With the mix of these three elements the answers of God are released.

I am now in my early sixties—"young old" according to some sociologists. It's the season of life when you put your dermatologist on speed dial, as there always seems to be a new spot that needs to be looked at by a set of professional eyes.

This morning I went to see my speed-dial buddy to examine two recent growths. I'd done a search online to attempt my own diagnosis, comparing pictures on websites with what I was seeing in the mirror. My tendency was to think the worst: some form of skin cancer, but what did I know? I needed the professional to give me his expert opinion.

Fortunately, this time it was nothing serious. One was a wart and the other was a precancerous growth. Both were dispatched with several shots from a freeze bottle.

At this season of life we are very aware that we are just one doctor's visit away from a life-changing diagnosis that will bring a new faith trial with much more serious consequences than praying for cars, houses, or bookcases. As I drove to my doctor this morning, I was reviewing some of the promises that give me comfort in times like these, especially during this season of life when many of our friends are receiving that dreaded word from their doctor.

I will lead the blind by ways they have not known,
　　along unfamiliar paths I will guide them;
I will turn the darkness into light before them
　　and make the rough places smooth.
These are the things I will do;
　　I will not forsake them. (Isaiah 42:16)

My sheep listen to my voice; I know them, and they follow me. I give them eternal life, and they shall never perish; no one can snatch them out of my hand. My Father, who has given them to me, is greater than all; no one can snatch them out of my Father's hand. I and the Father are one. (John 10:27-30)

Surely I am with you always, to the very end of the age. (Matthew 28:20)

I am the resurrection and the life. He who believes in me will live, even though he dies; and whoever lives and believes in me will never die. Do you believe this? (John 11:25-26)

Regardless of good news or earth-shattering, gut-wrenching, worst-case-scenario news, I do know that my God is on the throne of His universe and that nothing takes Him by surprise. Nothing is allowed to touch me without first passing through the filter of His good and perfect will for me.

In one sense one's entire life is preparation for the final act of faith when we look death in the eye and realize, *I'm going through to the other side.* Life is watching God prove Himself faithful to all of His promises, and that gives us hope for the promise of the resurrection from the dead. As Paul puts it,

If the dead are not raised, then Christ has not been raised either. And if Christ has not been raised, your faith is futile; you are still in your sins. Then those also who have fallen asleep in Christ are lost. If only for this life we have hope in Christ, we are to be pitied more than all men. (1 Corinthians 15:16-19)

One of the names for God revealed in the Old Testament is El Shaddai, God Almighty, which literally means, "the All-Sufficient One." He is sufficient for our every need. He is one who calls things into being that do not exist. He is not a God of probabilities or possibilities. He is God Almighty. Nothing is impossible for Him! Nothing is even difficult for Him. We are not like the unbelieving Israelites who "spoke against

God, saying, 'Can God spread a table in the desert?'" (Psalm 78:19). In the wilderness that is sometimes our lives, God can spread a lavish, full table for us, for, as the Omnipotent One, He is able to do whatever He wants. This is the Lord we know and love. This is the Lord who promises never to leave us and always to care for us.

The trustworthy character of God stands behind His promises. He is holy and true. He cannot lie or go back on His promises. He is faithful and will continue to be faithful, worthy of our trust. Therefore, "since we have these promises, dear friends, let us purify ourselves from everything that contaminates body and spirit, perfecting holiness out of reverence for God" (2 Corinthians 7:1). As a response to His wonderful promises we should pursue personal purity with our whole hearts. We strive to live a life honoring to Him because He has done so much for us. A God-honoring life flows from a grateful heart.

Chief Crowfoot was a Canadian Blackfoot Indian chief who lived near Alberta. In 1885 there was a large Indian uprising, the Saskatchewan Rebellion, but Chief Crowfoot led his people in a path of peace; they did not join the rebellion. As a token of the Canadian government's appreciation for his help, Chief Crowfoot was given a lifetime free pass to ride on the Trans-Canadian Railroad. Crowfoot acknowledged the receipt of the free pass by putting it in a leather pouch, which he hung around his neck. He died with the pouch around his neck, never having ridden on the railroad once!

The promises of God are like that lifetime railroad pass.

They are given to be used, not to be stored for future reference. They are given to be believed, trusted, tried, and proved. May we launch out into the adventure of pleading the promises of God in prayer. May we see Him glorify Himself as He does "immeasurably more than all we ask or imagine, according to his power that is at work within us" (Ephesians 3:20).

Appendix

The following is a list of promises compiled by topic.

ANSWERS TO PRAYER
1 Kings 18:37
Psalm 34:4
Psalm 37:4
Psalm 50:15
Psalm 86:7
Jeremiah 33:3
Luke 11:9-10
John 16:24
Philippians 4:6-7
James 5:15-16
1 John 5:14-15

ASSURANCE OF SALVATION
Isaiah 12:2
John 10:27-30
John 14:16-17
Romans 8:35-39
Ephesians 1:12-14
Ephesians 4:30
Philippians 1:6
1 Peter 1:5
1 John 5:11-13
2 John 1:2

COMFORT FROM GOD
Psalm 23:4
Psalm 27:10
Psalm 51:17
Psalm 55:22
Psalm 103:13-14
Isaiah 40:31
Isaiah 42:3
Isaiah 43:2
Isaiah 50:7
Matthew 5:4
Matthew 11:28-30
Matthew 28:20
Romans 8:28
2 Corinthians 1:3-4
1 Peter 5:6-7

FAITH
Psalm 5:11
Psalm 32:10
Psalm 118:8-9
Proverbs 29:25
Matthew 21:21-22
Mark 5:36
Mark 9:23-24
Mark 11:22-24
Romans 8:31
Ephesians 2:8-9
Hebrews 6:12
Hebrews 11:6
Hebrews 13:6
1 John 5:4

FORGIVENESS OF SIN
2 Chronicles 7:14
Psalm 32:5-6
Psalm 103:12
Isaiah 1:18
Isaiah 55:6-7
Matthew 6:14
Acts 10:43
2 Corinthians 5:17
Hebrews 8:12
1 John 1:9

GIVING
Psalm 112:5
Proverbs 3:9-10
Proverbs 11:24-25
Proverbs 19:17
Proverbs 28:27
Malachi 3:10
Matthew 6:1-4
Luke 6:38
Luke 14:12-14
Luke 16:9
2 Corinthians 8:12
2 Corinthians 9:6
2 Corinthians 9:8-11
1 Timothy 6:17-19

GUIDANCE
Psalm 32:8
Proverbs 3:5-6
Proverbs 16:3
Proverbs 21:5
Isaiah 30:21
Isaiah 40:11
Isaiah 42:16
Isaiah 45:2-3

Jeremiah 29:11
John 16:13
Romans 12:1-2
James 1:5

HEAVEN
Zechariah 2:10
Matthew 5:3
Matthew 5:10
John 6:51
John 14:2-3
Colossians 3:4
1 Thessalonians 4:16-17
Hebrews 9:28
Hebrews 10:37
1 John 3:2

LOVE AND CARE OF GOD
Job 23:10
Psalm 103:17
Nahum 1:7
Matthew 6:31-33
Matthew 10:29-31
John 14:21
John 15:9-10
Romans 5:8
Romans 8:32
1 Corinthians 10:13
Hebrews 12:11
1 Peter 5:7

MEDITATION
Joshua 1:8
Psalm 1:2-3
Psalm 19:14
Psalm 37:31
Psalm 63:6-8

Psalm 119:11
Psalm 119:97-99
Psalm 119:130
Psalm 119:147-149
Psalm 119:165

OBEDIENCE
Deuteronomy 4:39-40
Job 17:9
Psalm 119:57-58
Proverbs 1:32-33
Proverbs 16:7
Isaiah 1:19
Matthew 5:19
Luke 6:46-48
John 14:21,23
John 15:5
John 15:10-12
1 John 3:21-22

PATIENCE AND PERSEVERANCE
Psalm 27:14
Psalm 37:7
Isaiah 40:31
Romans 2:7
Romans 5:3-5
1 Corinthians 15:58
Galatians 6:9-10
Hebrews 10:35-36
James 1:2-4
James 5:7-8
2 Peter 3:8-9

PEACE
Exodus 33:14
Psalm 85:8
Psalm 119:165

Isaiah 26:3
Matthew 11:28-29
John 14:27
Romans 5:1
Romans 8:6
Colossians 3:15
1 Peter 3:9-11

POWER OF GOD
1 Chronicles 29:11
Job 42:2
Psalm 50:9-12
Psalm 115:3
Psalm 147:5
Isaiah 40:25-26
Isaiah 45:2-3
Jeremiah 27:5
Jeremiah 32:17,27
Luke 1:37
Ephesians 3:20-21
1 John 4:4

PROTECTION OF GOD
2 Chronicles 16:9
Psalm 5:11-12
Psalm 20:7
Psalm 27:1-3
Psalm 34:7
Psalm 46:1
Psalm 68:5
Psalm 73:23
Psalm 84:11
Psalm 91:5-8
Isaiah 41:10
Jeremiah 17:7-8
Romans 8:31
2 Thessalonians 3:3

PROVISION

Psalm 23:1
Psalm 34:9-10
Psalm 37:25
Psalm 69:33
Psalm 72:13
Psalm 95:6-7
Psalm 111:5
Proverbs 13:4
Matthew 6:33
Mark 10:29-30
2 Corinthians 9:8
Philippians 4:19

RELATIONSHIPS

Proverbs 16:7
Ecclesiastes 4:9-10
Luke 6:35-37
Romans 12:17-20
Romans 14:1-4
Romans 15:7
Ephesians 4:2-3
Ephesians 4:15
Ephesians 4:29-32
Ephesians 6:1-3
1 Peter 3:7
1 Peter 3:8-9

RESURRECTION

Psalm 49:15
Isaiah 26:19
Daniel 12:2-3
Matthew 22:30
Matthew 25:31-34
Luke 14:14

John 5:25,28-29
John 11:25-26
John 14:19
1 Corinthians 15:42-44
2 Corinthians 4:14

REWARDS

Jeremiah 17:10
Matthew 6:4
Matthew 10:42
Mark 10:29-30
Luke 14:14
John 12:26
1 Corinthians 15:58
2 Corinthians 5:10
Ephesians 6:7
Colossians 3:23-24
2 Timothy 4:8
Hebrews 6:10

SALVATION AND ETERNAL LIFE

John 1:12
John 3:16
John 5:24
John 6:47
John 20:31
Acts 16:31
Romans 6:22-23
Romans 10:9
Romans 10:13
Titus 1:3
Titus 3:4-7
1 John 2:25
Revelation 3:20

Bibliography

Clark, Samuel (1684-1750). *Precious Bible Promises.* New York: Grosset and Dunlap.

Gill, A. L. *God's Promises for Your Every Need.* Dallas: C&D International, 1981.

Lockyer, Herbert. *All the Promises of the Bible.* Grand Rapids: Zondervan, 1962.

Richards, Larry. *Daybreak Promises for Believers.* Grand Rapids: Zondervan, 2012.

Spurgeon, Charles (1834-1892). *Faith's Checkbook.* New Kensington, Pennsylvania: Whitaker House.

Viening, Edward. *The Zondervan Topical Bible.* Grand Rapids: Zondervan, 1969.

Notes

INTRODUCTION

1. Samuel Clark, quoted in J. I. Packer, *Knowing God* (Downers Grove, IL: InterVarsity Press, 1973), 103–104.
2. Packer, *Knowing God,* 103–104.

CHAPTER TWO

1. J. I. Packer, *Knowing God* (Downers Grove, IL: InterVarsity Press, 1973), 114–115.
2. Henry C. Thiessen, *Lectures in Systematic Theology* (Grand Rapids: Eerdmans, 1979), 87.
3. John MacArthur, *Ephesians,* MacArthur New Testament Commentary (Chicago: Moody Press, 1986), 30.
4. Warren Myers, "The Devotional Use of Scripture for Applications, Guidance and Promise-Claiming" (unpublished paper).
5. Myers, "Devotional Use of Scripture."
6. Herbert Lockyer, *All the Promises of the Bible* (Grand Rapids: Zondervan, 1962), 18–19.

CHAPTER THREE

1. Martin Luther, quoted in Robert Foster, *The Navigator* (Colorado Springs: NavPress, 1983), 71.
2. Charles Spurgeon, quoted in A. W. Tozer, *Let My People Go: The Life of Robert A. Jaffray* (Harrisburg, PA: Christian Publications, 1947), 56.
3. William R. Moody, *The Life of Dwight L. Moody* (Murfreesboro, TN: Sword of the Lord, 1900), 164.
4. Moody, *The Life of Dwight L. Moody,* 362.
5. Moody, *The Life of Dwight L. Moody,* 491.
6. Dwight L. Moody, quoted in Herbert Lockyer, *All the Promises of the Bible* (Grand Rapids: Zondervan, 1962), 6.
7. R. A. Torrey, quoted in *Frontier Focus,* 1, no. 1 (January 1991): 3.

8. Geraldine Taylor, *Behind the Ranges: The Life-Changing Story of J. O. Fraser* (Chicago: Moody Press, 1964), 146–147.
9. Tozer, *Let My People Go*, 96.
10. Howard and Geraldine Taylor, *Hudson Taylor's Spiritual Secret* (Chicago: Moody Press, 1932), 14.
11. Taylor and Taylor, *Hudson Taylor's Spiritual Secret,* 18.
12. Taylor and Taylor, *Hudson Taylor's Spiritual Secret,* 54.
13. Taylor and Taylor, *Hudson Taylor's Spiritual Secret,* 189.
14. Taylor and Taylor, *Hudson Taylor's Spiritual Secret,* 199.
15. Taylor and Taylor, *Hudson Taylor's Spiritual Secret,* 247.
16. Albert Sims, *An Hour With George Müller* (Grand Rapids: Zondervan, 1990), 25–27.
17. Betty Lee Skinner, *Daws: The Story of Dawson Trotman* (Grand Rapids: Zondervan, 1974), 40.
18. Skinner, *Daws*, 63.
19. Lorne Sanny, *How to Spend a Day in Prayer* (Colorado Springs: NavPress, 1981).
20. Lorne Sanny, quoted in the *Dear Staff Newsletter*, October 25, 1991, 1.
21. Sanny, *Dear Staff Newsletter,* 2–3.

CHAPTER FOUR
1. Norval Hadley, *Powerful Prayer Principles—Prevailing Prayer* (Pasadena, CA: International Intercessors, 1987).
2. Charles Spurgeon, quoted in Herbert Lockyer, *All the Promises of the Bible* (Grand Rapids: Zondervan, 1962), 55–56.
3. Spurgeon, quoted in Lockyer, *All the Promises of the Bible,* 51.

CHAPTER FIVE
1. George Mueller, quoted in Albert Sims, *An Hour with George Müller*, (Grand Rapids: Zondervan, 1990), 25.
2. Albert Sims, *An Hour With George Müller*, 34.
3. Bill Mills, *The Language of the Heart* (New Lenox, IL: Leadership Resources International, 1992), 129.
4. J. O. Fraser, quoted in Geraldine Taylor, *Behind the Ranges: The Life-Changing Story of J. O. Fraser* (Chicago: Moody Press, 1964), 152.
5. A. W. Tozer, *That Incredible Christian* (Wheaton, IL: Tyndale House, 1964), 28.

CHAPTER SIX

1. Ken L. Sarles, "A Theological Evaluation of the Prosperity Gospel," *Bibliotheca Sacra,* October 1986, 329–330.
2. Warren Myers, "The Devotional Use of Scripture for Applications, Guidance and Promise-Claiming" (unpublished paper).
3. John MacArthur, *Ephesians,* MacArthur New Testament Commentary (Chicago: Moody Press, 1986), 73.
4. MacArthur, *Ephesians,* 247.
5. J. O. Fraser, quoted in Geraldine Taylor, *Behind the Ranges: The Life-Changing Story of J. O. Fraser* (Chicago: Moody Press, 1964), 155–156.
6. Warren Myers, "The Devotional Use of Scripture for Applications, Guidance and Promise-Claiming" (unpublished paper).

CHAPTER SEVEN

1. The entire world has always been on God's heart. See also Isaiah 49:6; Matthew 28:19-20; Acts 1:8; 13:46-47; Revelation 7:9.
2. Arthur T. Pierson, *George Müller of Bristol* (Grand Rapids: Kregel, 1999), 170.
3. J. O. Sanders, quoted in a series of articles on prayer duplicated by The Navigators, Vienna, Austria, 1980.

CONCLUSION

1. J. I. Packer, *Knowing God* (Downers Grove, IL: InterVarsity Press, 1973), 238.

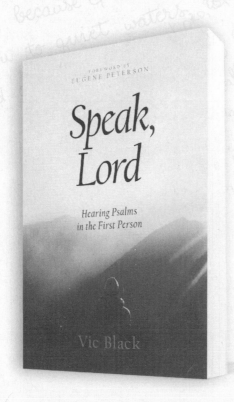

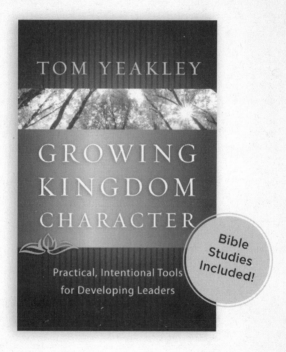